Southeast Asians Speak Out

Hope & despair in many lands

Southeast Asians Speak Out

Hope & despair in many lands

Barbara & Leon Howell

FRIENDSHIP PRESS • NEW YORK

PHOTO CREDITS

Page 14 by Koson Srisang
Pages 16, 49, 55, 71 and 107 by Leon Howell
Pages 22, 31, 33, 42 and 97 by Barbara Howell
Page 38 by Housing and Development Board, Singapore
Page 57 by Komol Chayawadna
Page 75 by Haney Howell

Library of Congress Cataloging in Publication Data

Howell, Barbara, comp.
Southeast Asians speak out.

Includes bibliographical references.
CONTENTS: The people: Koyama, K. Buddhist not Buddhism. Srisang, K. Free and compassionate. Rigos, C. To be Filipino. Danuriko, K. Profile of an Indonesian. Ali, S. M. No place to go.–The setting.–The places: Salonga, J. The Philippines under martial law. Sivaraksa, S. Thailand; the move away from military dictatorship. Than, U. K. Burma; interchange and identity. Hui L. M. Malaysia; race relations and economics. Morrow, T. H. Vietnamese women and the struggle for peace. Ann, L. S. Southeast Asia: The Economic Dimension. Lelyveld, J. U.S. in Southern Asia. [etc.]

1. Asia, Southeastern–Addresses, essays, lectures.
I. Howell, Leon, joint comp. II. Title.
DS504.5.H68 959 75-2130
ISBN 0-377-00025-6

Printed in the United States of America

CONTENTS

Introduction 7

THE PEOPLE 9

Buddhist Not Buddhism – Kosuke Koyama 10

Free and Compassionate – Koson Srisang 12

To Be Filipino – Cirilo A. Rigos 18

Profile of an Indonesian - Karel W. Danuriko 21

No Place to Go – S. M. Ali 25

THE SETTING – Barbara and Leon Howell 29

THE PLACES 44

The Philippines Under Martial Law – Senator Jovite Salonga 45

Thailand: The Move Away from Military Dictatorship – Sulak Sivaraksa 51

Burma: Interchange and Identity – U Kyaw Than 59

Malaysia: Race Relations and Economics – Lim Mah Hui 67

Vietnamese Women and the Struggle for Peace – Tue Hien Morrow 72

Southeast Asia: The Economic Dimension – Lee Soo Ann 78

U.S. in Southern Asia – Joseph Lelyveld 82

THE RELIGIONS 90

The Religions of Southeast Asia – Alan Thomson 91

Glimpses of the Church in Southeast Asia – Lee Soo Jin 100

Notes on Christian Identity in Asia Today – Feliciano V. Carino . . 112

The Church in Indonesia – Barbara Howell 117

APPENDIX A: Map of Southeast Asia 126

APPENDIX B: Southeast Asia at a Glance. 128

APPENDIX C: Population and Per Capita Income in Southeast Asian Countries 129

NOTES 130

INTRODUCTION

In 1954, as the French were being driven out of Vietnam by the Vietnamese, President Dwight D. Eisenhower is reported to have asked, "If we lost Vietnam and Malaya, how would we in the free world hold the rich empire of Indonesia?"[1]

Eisenhower resisted considerable pressure to intervene militarily on behalf of the French. But his remark illustrates a problem: for too long the United States has viewed the nations and peoples of Southeast Asia only out of an economic concern, rather than out of a desire to know and understand them.

In this book a number of writers from Southeast Asia speak out on the issues that shape their lives. For Americans, to whom Southeast Asia has existed largely as an extension of our concern over the war in Vietnam, the way these writers express their feelings, describe their nations and their problems, should do much to broaden our understanding of a region rich in history, diverse in culture, buffeted by problems and promises of which we know too little.

This book is divided into four parts. "The People" gives several Southeast Asians a chance to introduce themselves. "The Setting," written by the editors, offers some background on the region. "The Places" provides the views of citizens of five different nations on one key issue in their country. It also contains an economic overview of Southeast Asia and, because the book is designed basically for an American audience, includes an essay on U.S. presence in Southern Asia. "The Religions" has a general discussion of the rich spiritual traditions of Asian nations, then three specific articles on the Christian church.

Because of space limitations, little attention has been given to Indochina. Most readers of this book know of several excellent books and articles concerning Indochina. We are also missing an article on Indonesia, the largest and richest nation in Southeast Asia. The author, who had planned to discuss the problem of foreign investment in an Indonesia seeking to use its natural resources to overcome the deep poverty of its people, decided shortly before publication that the subject was too politically risky to address in a public forum. His fears are justified. At least one of the writers presented in this book, and at least two people quoted inside, are detained by government authorities as this book goes to press.

We do not attempt a systematic presentation of the history and current situations in Southeast Asia. A number of excellent resources—encyclopedias, picture books, general introductions, scholarly volumes—already exist for that purpose. The thirteen Asians writing here are sharing some of the things with which they wrestle in their daily lives. And from them we learn something of what it means to be alive in Southeast Asia today, caught at the intersection of hope and despair.

THE PEOPLE

The durian is a large greenish fruit, in appearance something like a prickly volleyball. Malaysians, Singaporeans and Indonesians anticipate the durian season with an intensity far surpassing Georgians and their peaches or New Englanders and their apples. Foreigners visiting the region find the durian fascinating, but its taste, to say the least, has to be acquired.

Dennis Bloodworth begins his always intriguing discussion of the Southeast Asia he knows in *An Eye for the Dragon* with a discussion on the durian.

He offers a long and weighty dictionary description of the *Durio Zibethinus*, noted for "its delicious flavour and its offensive odour. . . ." "Now you have been told all about the durian," Bloodworth observes, "and you know nothing. For you have neither smelled nor tasted it. . . .But men cheat and steal and fight over durians, as I know, for a big durian tree overhangs my garden in Singapore, and every year thieves smash down the fence to get at the stinking fruit."[2]

In "The Setting" some attempt will be made to set the historical stage for this book. But taken by itself, the dry bones of that outline mean nothing. Southeast Asia is people. Three hundred million human beings who walk and sing—who know joy, pain, fear and hope—who breathe and taste. Before thinking too much about the theology, the ideology, the topography and the archeology, let us begin at the beginning. Southeast Asia is people.

To know a Thai, a Burmese, an Indonesian, a Vietnamese, a Filipino, is to bring flesh and blood to what may otherwise appear as remote as the back side of the moon.

Kosuke Koyama affirms that "ist" comes before "ism." And then several people of Southeast Asia tell us who they are.

BUDDHIST NOT BUDDHISM

Kosuke Koyama

For eight years I lived in Thailand, a land of Theravada Buddhism. Thai Buddhism is, perhaps, the purest form of Buddhism practiced in the world today. Have you been to Bangkok? If you have, you must have seen some of the 240,000 monks of the kingdom on the streets of that bustling modern city. The monks live as though no change has taken place in the world for the last 2,500 years.

When I first went to Thailand, I had a rather negative view of Buddhism there. I felt that Buddhism did not have much of a future and was probably passing out of the thoughts of many millions in Southeast Asia. Since life had become increasingly modernized and secularized, that ancient religion of "detachment" and "tranquility" was bound to diminish. So I did not pay much attention to it.

However, after three years had passed, I had to revise my view of Buddhism in Thailand in a radical way. As my relationship with Buddhist friends increased and my language comprehension grew, I came to realize that what really matters is not a set of doctrines called Buddhism, but *people* who live according to the doctrine of the Buddha, or I should say who are trying to live according to the doctrine of the Buddha. Accordingly, my interest shifted from Buddhism to Buddhist people.

Soon I found that the study of *ist* is far more interesting and exciting than that of *ism.* I carefully observed Buddhists and to my surprise found many similar things between them and myself. One day I said to myself: "We are just alike. We want money. We want position. We want honor. We

---

Kosuke Koyama teaches at the University of Otago in Dunedin, New Zealand. He is also a writer–author of *Waterbuffalo Theology* and *Pilgrim or Tourist*–and former editor of *South East Asia Journal of Theology.* He has served as missionary from Japan to Thailand and as executive director of the Association of Theological Schools in South East Asia, living in Singapore. This article is reprinted by permission from *Waterbuffalo Theology,* copyright Orbis Books, Maryknoll, New York 10545.

are both concerned about ourselves. We are failing to practice what the Buddha or Christ commanded. We are quick in judging others and very slow in judging ourselves!" Comparisons on the level of Buddh*ist* and Christ*ian* often produce an embarrassing result. On the contrary, we can be well sheltered when we engage in the comparison between Buddh*ism* and Christ*ianity*. Here Christians frequently launch into "the defense of the right doctrines" so passionately and energetically that they become Christ*ianity* and cease to be Christ*ians*.

One can study Buddhism in school. Some will even study the Pali language in order to read the original Buddhist canon. One must not minimize the importance in understanding the ancient document of faith. But, again, here is something we must not forget: Buddhism does not feel hungry even if it does not eat for many centuries. Buddhism does not sweat even if it is placed under the hot tropical sun. Buddhism does not want to sell a bicycle and buy a motorcycle instead. Buddhism does not suffer from flood and drought. A Buddhist, on the contrary, is different. A Buddhist complains, laughs, grieves, sweats, suffers, thirsts and hungers–*for he is a man.*

When a man is a Buddhist, he does not cease to be a man. When a man is a Moslem, he does not cease to be a man. When a man is a Christian, he does not cease to be a man. A man does not cease to be "man." He does not become either an angel or a devil. By the grace of God, man remains man!

Man has many needs and drives: emotional, physical, intellectual, spiritual–all combined in a wonderful kind of unity. This "wonderful kind of unity," however, becomes from time to time seriously sick. Then man is paralyzed. Man is *homo aeger* (sick man) says Augustine. Yes, he is sick, yet he is unusual, wonderful and inspiring! What a great complex creature he is! Because he is so complex, man has always been a puzzle to man himself. It is easier for us to understand a lion or an elephant than to understand man himself. There are many doctrines, both helpful and harmful, about man. But even the best of all doctrines is not identical with the living man whom we see everyday, everywhere. If one of the doctrines on man had been adequate to explain him to himself, then, to use theological terminology, the "incarnation" would not have been necessary. Instead of the costly incarnation, God becoming man and dwelling amongst us, God might just as well have sent some wonderful doctrine about man. The best of all the good doctrines cannot compete with the one fact of God's incarnation in Jesus Christ.

Now, man is, according to the Bible, the "image of God." This is a great doctrine about man. Throughout the history of the Christian church, this doctrine has been actively at work. (Although I wish it worked more energetically!) Whenever the church opens her mouth on the issue of the "dignity of man," this doctrine of the "image of God" has been the point of departure. But this doctrine, in short, must not remain simply a doctrine. It must become integrated into our appreciation of men with whom we come in contact everyday. The "idea" of cold tea will not quench our thirst. It is, no doubt, a good theory for quenching our thirst, but theory cannot become effective until it is acted upon. When the "idea" of cold tea becomes actualized in ice cubes and a brown colored liquid called tea, then it can be drunk and will stop our thirst. So it is with the doctrine of the "image of God." It has to become, in each given situation, some sort of "ice cubes and brown colored liquid." That is to say, it must be actualized in man-to-man relationships if it is to display its dynamic and real power.

We are bound by all kinds of doctrines. Our interest is always on the side of *ism* rather than *ist.* Excessive interest in *ism* brings forth a disastrous situation which may be called the tyranny of doctrines. We tend to look at other persons through "doctrinally-trained" eyes. So we become experts in quick pronouncements of judgment upon others. When "doctrinally-trained eyes" say, "Now, master, this woman has been caught in adultery, in the very act. According to the Law, Moses commanded us to stone such women to death!" (John 8:4), the "incarnate-eyes" look in the *different direction.* "Jesus stooped down and began to write with his finger in the dust on the ground" (v.6). *Ism* and *ist* are related. Don't let *ism* walk alone!

FREE AND COMPASSIONATE

Reflections of a Thai

Koson Srisang

"I dreamed that a wise man handed me an inkpot," my mother recently recounted during a family reunion. "A month or two later," she continued, "I found out that I had conceived my first child."

It was a moonlit summer evening in the village house compound in

---

Koson Srisang teaches at the Thailand Theological Seminary in Chiangmai, Thailand. He holds degrees in educational administration from the University of Minnesota, and an M.A. and Ph.D. in Ethics and Society from the University of Chicago. Teacher, student work director and organizer of conferences, Koson has also edited and contributed to many works; his book *Thai Kingship: A Synthesis of the Thai Political and Religious Traditions* was in preparation in 1974.

Northeast Thailand where I was born three dozen years ago. My mother turned toward me, then paused to spew out the betel nuts she had been chewing. "I am sure that's why you have become a professor," she concluded.

"I would say of all the ten children I had carried, Koson's delivery was the toughest. Isn't that right, Father?"

My sixty-year old father nodded agreement. "The birth of the first child is always difficult," he said with an air of tested wisdom. "As a new father, I was so excited that I could not do a thing," he confessed. We all laughed. "If it were not for Uncle Yum and Tit Aw, the quack doctors, I don't know how you could have come out." He turned to me with a smile.

Mother and father continued to recount the birth stories of their children. Their eyes were bright, their voices clear when they told of those seven of us who are still living. But they were obviously sad–and we were too–when they told of the three who died young, not an uncommon experience for a family far from hospitals living in a village with no electricity or running water. "But by now," my mother said in a clear voice, sitting straight, "I am sure my three children must have been born again somewhere."

She was sure because in all her years she has never ceased praying for their good rebirth whenever she made merit in the Buddhist tradition, be it giving food to the monks or alms to the needy, poor as she herself is.

That is my mother: illiterate, wise and compassionate. I remember back to 1962 when I was preparing to leave for graduate study at the University of Minnesota on a Fulbright scholarship. She sought a moment when we could be alone. I knew she had something very important to say to me. I listened well, like a good son. She whispered, "Can't you walk to America instead of going by the 'flying boat' [her term for airplane] ? It's too risky going that way."

In mother's universe walking is not only the most reliable mode of movement but also the way by which you can observe things and see people best. She had no idea where that place called "America" was. I hugged her, tears running, and assured her: "Mother, I will take care of myself good, okay? You just take care of yourself and father and the kids. I will be back in no time. When it rains the next time, I will be home." She smiled, reluctantly I knew.

That is my mother, who pays minute attention to the events around her, particularly those which concern her and her family. I used to ask her what time of day I was born. "Oh, I remember exactly," she said. "It was just the time when our oxen and buffaloes were coming in from the field."

Clocks and watches were nonexistent in her world then. Time was, and still is to a great extent, measured by rain, harvest, the roosters' crow, the movement of the oxen and buffaloes, the great sermon which comes once a year.

Koson (right) and his father, August, 1966 at Don Muang airport, on the day Koson and his family left for the U.S.A.

My father is different. Although he too never went to school, he taught himself to read and to sign his name. Grandfather was sort of a roving *nak leng,* a man who possessed something a sociologist like Max Weber would call charisma. But he is more. He is kind to his own men and those treated unjustly, but fiercely cruel to his enemies and those who are unfair. He plans and executes thefts, and sometimes even robbery. Something of a Robin Hood, a *nak leng* usually takes from the crooked rich. A *nak leng* is believed to possess some sacred *mantras* (prayers or incantations to deities from the Hindu tradition) which provide immunity against guns and knives. But in order to maintain the *mantras'* sacredness, he must observe a set of strict disciplinary rules, such as refraining from eating certain kinds of fruit or snake and abstaining from sexual relations for three days before the execution of his plan.

Grandfather died when my father was a child, which prevented him from becoming as good a *nak leng.* But, like father, like son, as the saying goes in Thailand–and the United States. Father did learn from grandfather and developed some of his character.

He became what is known among villagers as *hoa maw,* someone gifted in speech and argument, particularly in defense of poor villagers against official authority whose seat of power is the capital. If a person is both *nak leng* and *hoa maw,* he would usually be elected village headman. Otherwise the two work together.

Because of his status as a *hoa maw,* father walked several times to the provincial capital. This came in handy when I needed him in 1952; what he did then turned out to be crucial in the unfolding drama of our family. Let me recount it to you briefly.

Shortly after the end of World War II, a terrible smallpox epidemic broke out in Thailand. Many of my friends died at that time, and I almost did. Not until after the epidemic ended did I begin school, at the age of nine. Four years later I graduated first from the fourth grade class.

Several options were then open to me. Having seen so much injustice and admiring how my father had been able to help so many people, I wanted to follow his example. Physically and psychically, I could not become a *nak leng,* having partaken much from my mother's compassionate nature. But I could probably become a *hoa maw.*

Three other choices were open for me. I could become a Buddhist novice, learning the Dhamma and become an abbot who would be able to help the villagers not only by preaching but also by leading them in community development, just as many great monks had done in the history of my village. Besides, if I so desired, I could resign later and return to lay life.

An attractive possibility would be to become a *maw lum,* an actor-singer whose duty it was to entertain. I had seen and admired many *maw lums.* A good and creative *maw lum* not only knew popularity but he could compose his own songs, songs which could become instructive, uplifting the quality of life and promoting justice.

Because they did not cost anything in cash–villagers in my area had little cash at the best of times, and droughts and World War II had brought poverty to our village–the first two were in fact the only options open to me for awhile.

The third possibility was to continue schooling to grade five and onward. Only one or two in the village had ever done this before. Once they had done so, they migrated away and rarely came to visit. Yet, one such person, Kru Prasan Prasarntri, suggested and encouraged this option.

Because it was, and still is, beyond compulsory education in Thailand, this was a costly alternative.

This is what my father wanted me to do. "Son, let us labor for a year or two and save up so that you can go to grade five. It will cost us at least 200 or 300 baht ($10 to $15). And now I have no money." The prospects were dim, but neither of us would give up, not yet anyway.

I had raised a hen, who was my friend, just like I took care of my father's buffalo, also a friend. Oh, I have many fond stories about these friends. The buffalo I watched was so understanding that, at the sound of my voice, he would do exactly what I asked. Unlike most buffaloes, he would never break into people's gardens, or eat the rice plants. My friend the buffalo was also my vehicle. When cholera killed him, I cried for days. Ceremonially I buried him, his whole big body. I could tell many more stories, but I shall resist the temptation. Back to my hen, and her nine chicks.

In order to try to continue in school, I reluctantly sold my hen and her nine chicks to an uncle who gave me ten baht (50¢) in return. Actually, I sold the chicks. I could not sell my friend the hen, so I gave her away. With that ten baht I began my further education. And it was always difficult. Many of mother's few inherited possessions also had to be "given away" to get the baht to keep me in school. Life was so difficult that I often swallowed my meals with tears.

In 1952 the educational office at the provincial capital announced a competitive exam for a government scholarship to a student entering the eighth grade. Typically, my head teacher received the announcement on Thursday; the application deadline was the next day. And in 1952 an old

School children in Koson's village going to class in the Wat (temple) area in background. The center of life in small traditional Thai villages, the Wat is the center for schooling, traditional medical work and religious and secular gatherings.

bus made the run from the school town to the provincial capital only once a week.

My father walked through the night Thursday in order to submit my application in time. Had he not been there before as a *hoa maw,* he would not have known where to go or what to do. The opportunity would have been lost. Thank goodness, I won that scholarship!

If it had not been for father's all-night walk that Thursday, I probably would have been forced to leave school. And the drama of our family would have been otherwise.

As a symbol of thanks and sharing, when I received the 600 baht ($30) scholarship money, I bought a buffalo for my father to replace the one which died a few years earlier. (That was an extraordinary event among the villagers, unexpectedly making me an instant celebrity there.) I was also able to share with my family in another way. I was able to assist my other brothers to continue their education, except the one next to me who had finished grade four before I won the scholarship. Now some of them are educated and have their own families.

Thank you, Father. Your *hoa maw* not only protected the interests of the villagers, but also promoted your children's well being.

That was the early part of my life, the formative years, the experiences which shaped my character, gave direction to my life. It has been some twenty years now since I graduated from my secondary school. What has happened to me, what I have done, in my adult years has largely been the unfolding drama whose plot had been conceived and laid out in the first seventeen years of my life.

I realize that I have been through my college and graduate school days in a simple spirit and with a single aim: to drink in compassion the cup of poverty and suffering of my people. And, God help me, to do what I can to help liberate them from their suffering, the suffering they have lived with for so long that they don't even think they can break it.

The spirit in which I have carried out this mission is that of common humanity. We are all human, equally human. No one has the right to treat another as less human; no one is more human than another. This spirit was born in me and nurtured through my childhood; my education and experiences as a Christian have furthered that conviction.

Let me give an example of the sense of mission I mention, the obligation I feel. An irrigation dam was built in my native village in Mahasarakham Province eight years ago. The government took land from villagers to build the dam; they were to be paid compensation. Eight years went by. In April, 1974, they still had not received word on when they could get the promised money. They consulted me during a visit to my home. Needless to say, I was very angry and knew that something had to be done.

It happened that I had organized, as acting director, the first student-faculty seminar on political issues at the Student Christian Center in Bangkok. In 1966 then Professor Sanya Dharmasakti had talked to the seminar, at my invitation, on "Ethics and National Development." He had become Prime Minister Sanya when the 1973 student demonstration forced the old and corrupt Thanom forces out of office. So I wrote to the new Prime Minister about the problem; three months later the farmers began to receive their money. I am still mad, however, that I had to write that letter.

I have definite plans to go back and help my people. The aim remains clear; the spirit grows even stronger. But this is no place to go into such details.

Even in my marriage and the raising of my family, the same attitudes prevail. Wannee, a trained teacher herself, and our two daughters have shared with me completely and willingly in dedicating our lives to such an aim and in such a spirit as stated before.

We know, of course, that our high hopes and pure intention may fall flat. But we do know. that insofar as we breathe, we will do our very best to follow our conviction, in faith and hope.

For we have seen that life is worth living only when it is free and compassionate. A personal view, of course, but one that sustains us.

TO BE FILIPINO

Cirilo A. Rigos

I belong to the Malay race. Perhaps I have some Chinese blood in my body. My name is Spanish; I think in Pilipino; I write in English.

I come from a country of about 115,800 square miles. The Philippines is larger than Great Britain and almost ten times the size of Belgium. We have 7,109 islands. We have eighty-eight dialects and *Pilipino* is our

Cirilo A. Rigos is pastor of the Cosmopolitan Church in Manila, Philippines. He became known to many Americans when he served as a mission consultant to the United Church Board for World Ministries. Among many special responsibilities, he is one of two Protestants on the national Church-Military Liaison Committee created after martial law was declared in 1972. Dr. Rigos is author of *Rebuilding Our Broken Faith* and *Christians and Revolution.*

national language. *Filipino* often means a Philippine citizen. While the Filipinos are being encouraged to speak Pilipino (in addition to their native dialects), English is actually our second language.*

Like other Orientals, we treasure the value of cohesiveness in the family. In spite of Western influences that put a premium on individualism, a typical Filipino considers the thinking and the feeling of the family–and even of the clan–before making a decision. The marriage between two people is often the marriage between two families. Aging parents fall into the care of one of the children.

We have a deep yearning for formal education. Parents sell or mortgage their properties if that is the only way to send their children to school. Only a few college students get married before graduation. Many of our medical doctors and nurses and, more recently, other professionals migrate to the United States and Canada where they can earn more.

We are a singing people. Restaurants and night clubs in Tokyo, Hong Kong, Singapore and other Asian cities import singers from the Philippines. But perhaps we are known best for our hospitality and our, sometimes excessive, gratitude.

During the New Stone Age, some Indonesians from the Asian mainland came to the Philippines leaving traces of their culture in the northern part of the country. The last migrating people arriving at our shores were the Malays from the southeastern part of the Asian continent. Between the twelfth and fourteenth centuries the Islamic influence from Arabia caused many Filipinos, notably those in the southern Philippines, to embrace that faith. Indian and Chinese words used in some of our native dialects reflect the earlier contact with those great nations.

While I am not so sure about the Chinese blood in my body, many of my friends have last names like Chan, Diao, Yang, Te and Go.

My homeland was invaded by Ferdinand Magellan, the Spanish explorer, in 1521, and he lost his life in Cebu. The Spanish colonialization which followed gave us our hispanized names and Roman Catholic faith. Today about 80 percent of our people are Roman Catholic.

Following the Spanish-American War in 1898, the United States annexed the Philippines. For more that two years Filipino guerrillas fought for independence against the Americans but were finally subdued by the Americans' superior arms. The new rulers promised that after a period of training for self-government Philippine independence would be granted.

The American regime in the Philippines was interrupted by the Japanese occupation of the country in December, 1942, immediately after the bombing of Pearl Harbor. General Douglas MacArthur promised before leaving the Philippines, "I shall return." And he did. In the early part of

*In common usage, the nation is referred to as the Philippines, the people as Filipino and the language encouraged be spoken as Pilipino.

1945, the American forces liberated us. On July fourth of the following year, amid the ruins of Manila, Philippine independence was granted in a simple but solemn ceremony.

The nation concentrated on rehabilitating itself, but the war's aftermath, and inexperience in governing, made the sailing rough. From 1948 to 1954 the uprising of the Huks (Hukbalahap–"People's Anti-Japanese Army")–often branded as Communists by the foreign press–sapped the energy of government authorities. The 1960's were characterized by a rising spirit of nationalism spearheaded by the students and a number of intellectuals. The early seventies witnessed the militancy of student demonstrations and the spread of anarchy. In September, 1972, the President felt it was necessary to place the country under martial law.

Martial law means the temporary curtailment of some of our liberties. This is necessary to save the country from being dominated by the subversives. Our President assures us that his government is not a dictatorship; it is constitutional authoritarianism. But, like other Filipinos, I pray that soon we may shift back to the normal processes of democracy.

We have been told that our economy has never been so good. We have an open-arm policy to foreign investors. The Japanese have become our foremost trading partner. The Philippine-Japan Treaty of Amity, Commerce and Navigation has opened the gates for more Japanese business to flood into the country. I am terribly concerned about the rapidly expanding Japanese economic empire in the Philippines.

American presence in the Philippines, especially the U.S. military bases, has long been a controversial subject. Many believe that such bases give us a measure of protection against foreign aggression. Others contend that we are exposed to danger precisely because of those bases. My overriding concern is for us as a people to be able to make our own decisions without pressure from anywhere. I have been a recipient of American hospitality and generosity. I have studied in American schools on American scholarships. But I refuse to become blind to the irritants in the Philippine-American relationship. The Americans are here to protect their interests, and we Filipinos protect ours. And when there is any conflict of interests, we remember the saying that in international politics there are no permanent friends, only permanent interests.

I am embarrassed by the fact that I know more about the Americans than about the Koreans. In fact, this is the situation in many parts of Asia. I would not be surprised if the Indonesians know the Dutch more than they know us; the Indians know the British more than the Burmese; the Vietnamese know the French more than the Thais. Of course, we are victims of historical events. But like many other Asians I refuse to remain a prisoner of the past. I long for an Asian community of nations that promotes understanding and unity among itself.

As a Filipino, I share in the vision of the New Society–a society where men and women are free and are responsible in the exercise of their freedom, free to seek the truth and zealous to preserve their liberties. It is a society where peace is based on justice and where the dignity of all, however lowly they may be, is truly respected.

As a Christian pastor, I enjoin church people and my fellow citizens to seek the will of God for us these days and to be aware that even our best understanding of his will may be tainted by our sin and prejudices; manifest our utmost concern for the cause of truth and justice; be generous in appreciating the good and courageous in condemning the wrong; and constantly to subject our judgments and decisions to the further scrutiny of the Spirit. I enjoin my colleagues to play the role of reconcilers but not at the cost of sacrificing our calling to be prophetic. And I enjoin everyone to cast their lot with the victims of oppression and injustice, even if it means facing their own crucifixion.

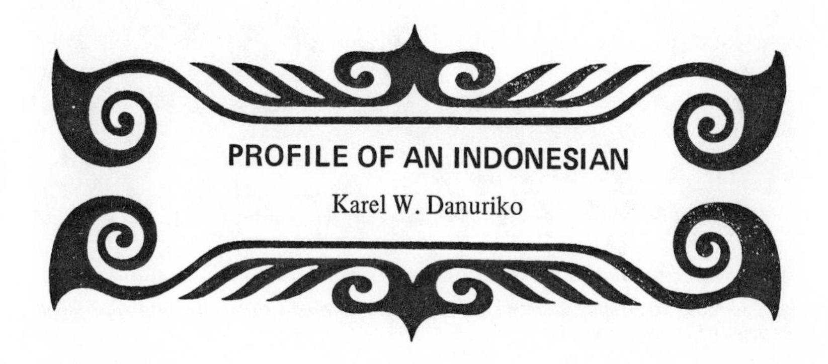

PROFILE OF AN INDONESIAN

Karel W. Danuriko

One dimension of an Indonesian dominantly colors any profile. Islam is the religion of 80 percent of the 130 million people in the Indonesian islands. The impact of being a Muslim could be traced almost everywhere, from the top office of government to the huts of the villager. It plays an important role in a Muslim's way of life, the philosophy of poor and rich, freedom and oppression, power and powerlessness, sickness and health.

The Indonesian who is a Muslim marks the day by a continuous routine of prayer five times a day. The first prayer takes place around 7 p.m., followed by morning prayer at about 4:45 a.m., again at noon, about 1:30 p.m. and around 6 p.m., right before the sun falls below the horizon. A Muslim's life flows consistently through the central stream of this religious agenda.

Islam is the "theme" of the song of life. To be poor, rich, sick, healthy, oppressed or free are only the symptoms, as if *tunes* of the song

Karel W. Danuriko is a key staff member of the Urban Industrial Mission Project of the Indonesian Council of Churches.

These terraced rice fields in Java, Indonesia, are common to all the Southeast Asian countries where rice is the basic food.

composing the rhythm of that song of life. Islam shapes and forms the life from birth to the end of life. Rigid and consistent performance of Islam is deeply planted in the roots of human body and mind; it composes a believer more than any other factor.

We Indonesians understand that the old Hinduism was chewed up and assimilated into Islam. Influential Dutch colonial systems and cultures, the Portuguese domination, times of British influence, the Japanese occupation, the movement to independence and freedom, modern technology and the Christian biblical influence are seen by the Muslim as enrichment of Islam itself.

Following is an interview with Mr. Sujana S. In a nation where the per capita annual income is less than $100 per year, he is a man of modest means. But many of his answers, as a faithful follower of Islam and a resident of Java–the island where perhaps 80 million Indonesians crowd together–could come from even top persons in the nation.

A young farmer, about twenty-nine, Sujana lives in West Java not far from Bandung city in a community of more than 25,000. Married with one child, he lives in a peasant house with his parents, two younger brothers and two buffaloes.

He has ownership of a portion of a rice field 150 square meters (about 1/25th an acre) in size, which averages about 500 kilograms (about 1,200 pounds) of rice per year in two planting sessions. The rice field is surrounded by a few banana, coconut and rambutan trees.

As the eldest of the family, Sujana is responsible for feeding all the mouths in the family. He does so by hard work: plowing the small land through the use of the buffaloes.

Although Sujana never finished primary school, he knows how to read and write Indonesian in the Roman script and Arabic used in Muslim instruction. His informal education in Muslim tradition was completed by visiting several "pesantren," where renown teachers discuss the practical theology of a true Muslim. While the lectures are often not academically sound. they provide guidelines in manners and Islam.

Sujana went a step further and traveled around Java and Sumatra in 1964-65 visiting holy graves of Muslim saints and seeking by praying, fasting and contemplation, the wisdom of life. Through the mediation of the saints he also sought to receive the supernatural power of *kebatinan*, the mystical conviction that empowers him to perform "miracles" such as healing the sick, quickening the growth of crops, helping the young to get the love of their intended wife or husband and helping businessmen to get loans.

After this informal education, Sujana was happy to serve his family and community. We had the following discussion in Jakarta.

What is the most central thing in your life?

I believe in Islam, so I focus my life on its performance and teach others or encourage them to perform the same Islam.

What does it mean to be poor?

Poor and rich are the will of Allah. Allah, the one God, regulates our life precisely like the tire that is rolling. Sometimes we are up and sometimes down. Poor means that we are to the ground, suppressed by the gravity of the tire: no food, no clothes, no power or recognition, no recreation or pleasure. In that situation, we call on Allah with an empty mouth. Allah will be greeted as if we are crying over the pain from striking our toes on a stone.

Rich is the opposite of being poor. We are in the air so we will greet Allah with a full mouth, like calling to Him while our mouth is filled with rice. But Allah organizes our ups and downs. In our downs, we are hoping. In our ups, we are grateful.

What does it mean to be in power?

Power belongs to Allah, the Almighty. All have the opportunity to be in power if Allah wants it. Government is the will of Allah to regulate the discipline in the world. He will change the bad guys with good guys periodically.

What do you think about the present government?

As a whole, it is good, better than during Sukarno's time (which lasted until 1966). Sukarno's mission as holder of Allah's power was replaced by General Suharto. There are plenty of corrupt officials among Suharto's officials but we pray that they will soon be changed for good guys.

Do you feel uneasy to criticize the government?

Not at all. But it is the matter of how and who. We have chosen people with special power to criticize. They are the ones to do that function. The spirit of our ancestors will never keep bad guys too long above us.

Are you proud of your government?

Sure, I am proud of the government, but I am prouder of my country, to be an Indonesian; at the most I am proud of being a Moslem. I have been chosen to be the servant of Allah.

Are you happy about foreign investment?

As a whole I am happy, because foreigners have more capital and have the skills to help the economy. We get some benefits, or at least the skills. Anyhow, I am not happy to hear they pay more to the white (foreign) staffs than to the Indonesians. It is rumored that a few Indonesian officials are getting richer and richer while they oppress their Indonesian subordinates. If the foreign system discriminates here I am sure someday people will protest again. Allah never allows oppressive systems to be everlasting.

What are the hopes you have for your family and yourself?

Better school opportunities, better medicine, cheaper clothes, cheaper radios, roads to the mountains and better mosques.

I hope that the government's development plan will be successful, but I am unhappy that it is so slow and that only those who live in big cities have more opportunity.

Anyhow, I have more hope in the wisdom and providence of Allah than in the promises made every day through news releases.

What do you know about other religions?

I have friends who are Christians. All religions are good because Allah wants them to exist as means to the end, which is Allah. No one has the right to proclaim that one religion is the best way because Allah chooses the best way for each of us. That should guide our interaction with other religions.

Good believers in various religions could go hand in hand in developing the nation. Myself will be very happy if Christians come around to my house and be my guests.

NO PLACE TO GO

S. M. Ali

More than a decade ago two other journalists and I shared an office in a weekly regional journal. An exciting venture when we arrived, the magazine deteriorated within a few years to a weak imitation of a better-known American weekend supplement.

Still committed to Asian journalism, we went our own ways, becoming involved in other, slightly bolder experiments. In mid-1974 the three of us had a chance in Manila to talk about our memories and our futures.

We found out that the Asia we had reported in the early 1960's had changed. We were less certain about our roles as journalists, about the function of regional reporting. And while we discussed concrete projects, we were probably unconsciously searching for a new direction to the kind of idealism that had moved us at the beginning of the sixties. It seemed an impossible exercise.

In retrospect, our conversation seems to illustrate the dilemma of a far broader group of Asians. Confronted by enormous socio-economic problems, the Asian leader, businessman, educator or writer remembers nostalgically the spirit of national effort widespread a decade ago. And he wonders if his own perspective is adequate for today.

I am almost but not quite from Southeast Asia. My country, now widely known to the world as Bangladesh, borders the region and may in the future have greater economic contact with Southeast Asia. But

---

S. M. Ali is one of the few Asian journalists to distinguish himself in regional journalism. A native of what is now Bangladesh, he has served as managing editor of the *Bangkok Post* and the *Hong Kong Standard,* roving foreign editor of the Singapore *New Nation* and worked on papers in both East and West Pakistan. After the bloody emergence of Bangladesh at the end of 1971, he spent much of 1972 in his homeland and produced the book *After the Dark Night: Problems of Sheikh Mujibur Rahman,* widely considered to be one of the most acute assessments of the problems and promises of Bangladesh.

geographically and historically it is part of the Indian subcontinent. My arrival in Hong Kong more than a decade ago was not without incident: Bangladesh was then part of Pakistan, ruled dictatorially by the military regime of General Ayub Khan. My passport had been impounded and it took special interceding with the Ministry of Interior to get it returned to me.

A full and busy decade passed; I traveled in the region and worked in Hong Kong, Bangkok and Singapore. In early 1972 I left Southeast Asia for about six months to live in my home country, Bangladesh, which had just emerged after the devastating war in 1971.

The day before I left for the Bangladesh capital of Dacca, a non-Asian friend asked for my impression of the "changes" that had occurred in Southeast Asia in the decade I had lived here.

So much went through my mind. Indonesia had rejected President Sukarno's free-wheeling excesses and was now governed by the less colorful General Suharto, who maintained his power with the military but tried to bring economic reform by using technocrats in the government. Poor Norodom Sihanouk in Cambodia, who had kept his country in peace as the Vietnam war raged around him, was in exile and Cambodia was in torment. Thailand was still a military dictatorship, but Field Marshal Thanom Kittikachorn existed on "borrowed time" (when I wrote an article with that title, Thai authorities banned me temporarily) while his deputy, General Prapas Charusathiara, went about making himself rich. Burma remained for the entire decade a country "gone underground."

This and much more went through my mind. But he was a newcomer to Asia. And I was at a loss to help him understand. So I gave him an innocuous answer that conveyed nothing of the dilemma and the uncertainty, the despair and frustration, which some of us can only share among ourselves.

How does one convey these feelings to people who do not know Asia? I suppose the root of the problem of communicating this uneasiness is our inability to understand what is happening now or to forecast what is likely to happen in the near future.

Some observers point to the trend toward more authoritarian governments, such as the martial law dictatorship of Marcos in the Philippines, as the wave of the future. Democracy was foisted off on Asians; their strongest need now is for stable leadership which permits orderly economic development.

But others witness the terrible society created by President Park Chung Hee in South Korea (Americans must wonder precisely what they fought for in the Korean War) and fear the excesses of unchecked power. Moreover, they witness the Thai struggle for democratic institutions and reject any easy suggestions that Asians naturally prefer autocratic states.

The Asian writer's dilemma in describing this region is made more difficult by a growing alienation from the forces which, in one way or another, become responsible for the changes in individual Asian countries. Singapore, often thought to be a social democracy, allows no press freedom, as editors jailed or papers arbitrarily closed illustrate.

But the newspaper reporter educated in the Western liberal tradition finds as do other educated Asians that he has contributed to the near extinction of the free press in Asia. As journalists, we failed to establish the relevance between liberal values and the causes of political instability in Southeast Asian countries. While we upheld the concept of a government responsibile to the people, while we defended a free press, economic challenges from the population explosion to income disparities continually corroded infant political institutions.

The Asian journalist derived strength from what a Filipino columnist, Juan T. Gatbonton, has described as the "inherent factionalism of national politics." And the reporter unwittingly played a part in creating a "democracy of stalemate" in which national decision-making almost came to a halt and economic pressures mounted. In such situations, here and there, "strongmen" appeared and took the power themselves, under the pretext of getting the decision-making process moving again. The Asian journalist was left without defenses. The free press fell by the wayside. More disturbing to many Asian journalists, it now appears clear that the free press as it is, say, in India today, or in the Philippines before martial law, had survived as an integral part of a political order that had lost its effectiveness, if not its validity.

The point is not easy to express. But it is clear that Asian journalists, Asian intellectuals in fact, must reexamine their own beliefs, their own commitments.

I have said that we are unable to say much about the future. But we do have an uneasy feeling that the situation may probably grow worse in the immediate future.

The key to our Asian crisis is economic. We watch as rising inflation has threatened the continued stability of political institutions in nations like Italy and even Great Britain with its history of free expression. We can hardly expect the forces of authoritarianism to loosen their hold on Myrdal's "soft states" in Asia.

Many experts predict that the continuing population explosion dooms millions in rural Asia to diminishing incomes for an indefinite period. If correct, we have to ask whether India's liberal democracy can meet the challenge. Could the Philippines, whose free-swinging politics have been circumscribed by martial law, meet the challenge better? Which way will poor countries like Sri Lanka and Bangladesh swing in the next few years?

We still feel that authoritarianism of the South Korean type cannot cope with the growing economic crisis of the Third World. Indistinguishable from naked fascism, personalized dictatorship usually becomes too isolated to perform its economic functions. And the inefficient and corrupt totalitarianism experienced by Thailand until late 1973 seems an exercise in futility.

It is just possible that authoritarian rulers in Singapore, Burma and perhaps even the Philippines will learn not only from the mistakes of their liberal predecessors but also from the more glaring blunders of people like Park in Korea, Thanom in Thailand and Pakistan's Ayub and Yahya Khan. They may learn (although that remains to be seen) that an administration does not become effective merely by stifling its opposition. And they may decide that real authority cannot be exercised without allowing some of the institutions through which the people speak to spring up again.

Is there a chance that in facing the tremendous challenge of the 1970's, in attempting to resolve the inner contradictions of the systems that support them, there authoritarian rulers may meet halfway those of us who are sometimes scorned as "liberal intellectuals?"

But, then, is such a development possible without a reexamination of our own beliefs and positions in the Asian scene?

The dilemma becomes a challenge. All said and done, we in Asia are already involved. We have no choice. We have no place to go.

Barbara and Leon Howell

THE SETTING

This is a book about Southeast Asia, a convenient descriptive phrase for Burma, Cambodia, Indonesia, Laos, Malaysia, the Philippines, Singapore, Thailand and Vietnam (North and South).*

Yet few of the 300 million residents of the region think of themselves as Southeast Asians. The term is contemporary, only dating back to World War II when Great Britain called its Asian headquarters just south of India on Ceylon the Southeast Asia Command. Nor is it precise. One Indonesian asks, "Southeast of what?"

Still, the area is distinctive. Its location in the heat and humidity of the equatorial tropics sets it off from the rest of Asia. Water has always been the bridge between the various peoples of Southeast Asia; of the ten nations listed only Burma and Laos do not open onto the calm South China Sea, often called Asia's Mediterranean. Great navigable rivers such as the Mekong, Irrawaddy and Chao Phraya, and smaller seas like Java and Celebes, increase the accessibility of the region. Neither the Latin

*A geographical definition of Southeast Asia would also include the tiny enclave of Brunei, wedged in between Malaysia's two states on northern Borneo. It is an oil-rich sultanate which continues to pay for a token British military presence. The more than 600,000 people on the 5,763 square miles of Timor which were controlled by Portugal are in a state of flux after the political upheaval in Portugal. Although a fairly strong sentiment for independence exists, the freed half of the island seems likely to join the Indonesian part of the island as part of Indonesia. In an economic but not a geographic sense the British crown colony of Hong Kong is often seen as part of Southeast Asia.

American or African tropics can be so easily reached, a mixed blessing to Southeast Asia.

Add ample rainfall from the semi-annual monsoons to tropical coasts and river deltas and the classic rice-growing region unfolds. People have always been drawn to the alluvial lowlands and the coastal plains. In Europe, high population clusters mean industry; in Southeast Asia dense population indicates agriculture, usually rice.

Southeast Asia contains about 1.6 million square miles of land (about half that of the United States) and in vast areas, such as the central jungle of the Malay peninsula, Burma's mountains, Indonesia's Sumatra and Irian Jaya, it seems underpopulated. But the amount of truly usable land for the agricultural economy is limited, and Southeast Asia is overpopulated in a truly demographic sense.

Too often Southeast Asia is approached from the vantage point of its colonial past–*French* Indochina; *British* Malaysia, Singapore and Burma; *Dutch* East Indies (Indonesia); *Spanish* (or American) Philippines. Or it is dissected by the scalpel of its two most important cultural antecedents, India and China. Surely the colonial period, as well as the Indo-Chinese transfusions, are important. But they should not be used as exclusive descriptions of the complex history and rich culture of the region.

A more obvious division for Southeast Asia occurs between mainland–Burma, Cambodia, Laos, Thailand and the Vietnams–and insular Southeast Asia–the Malay peninsula, Singapore, Indonesia and the Philippines. On the mainland people concentrated in river settlements; on the islands the major cities were usually coastal.

From North Vietnam's Red River valley, Burma's Irrawaddy delta and the Chao Phraya lowland in Thailand, people flowed north and south from China and Tibet. While clearly the Chinese racial strains, technically mongoloid, have intermingled with the predecessors to the Malays, a unified racial strain known as Malay spread. Early mastery of the boat propelled them to move across Indonesia, Malaysia, the Philippines and into Taiwan. (Various theories exist on the Malay's origins; it is known that the name comes from a town in Sumatra once called Melayu.)

The Southeast Asian subcontinent has been called the "land of the yellow robe"; monks by the thousands, head-shaven, wearing the common saffron robe, begging for their food, punctuate the flow of people in Burma, Laos, Cambodia and Thailand. Vietnam–which experienced 1,000 years of Chinese rule–reflects more the Chinese folk religion of Confucianism, family worship and Mahayana Buddhism.

The Malay peoples of the islands follow Islam overwhelmingly, with the exception of the Philippines where Roman Catholicism predominates (except for about five million fiercely independent Filipino Muslims known as Moros who live on the southern island of Mindanao and the Sulu Chain.

Another caution should be expressed. Differences within countries in both divisions are also great. As one of the major historians of Southeast Asia, D. G. E. Hall, has remarked: "The whole area has been described as a chaos of races and languages."[3]

For example: Indonesia's national language is basically Malay (called Bahasa Indonesia) but in the islands more than 25 languages and 250 dialects are spoken. Some Indonesian regional languages use Indian scripts, as do Burmese, Thai, Cambodian and Laotian. Arabic script superceded this in such places as Ajeh in northern Sumatra and Malaysia. But in Malaysia a Roman script has also been adopted, as it has for most of Indonesia, the Philippines and Vietnam, where Chinese ideographs once were employed.

UNCOVERING THE PAST

Hall has also called Southeast Asia "an anthropologist's paradise." In fact, systematic search into the past has barely begun in Southeast Asia; much of the region's prehistory remains covered in mystery as pervasive as the jungle growth hiding the magnificent ruins of Angkor Wat for four centuries. But enough has been exposed to change dramatically the thinking about Southeast Asia's history.

Excavations in Thailand, Malaysia, the Philippines, Vietnam and northern Australia in the past decade have challenged the conventional theories that civilization came to Southeast Asia in progressive "waves of

An Indonesian woman painstakingly uses hot wax to paint the first layer of a traditional batik.

culture" from better-known centers of development, especially China. Some now feel that *homo sapiens* may have emerged in Southeast Asia and not arrived by migration. Evidence in the form of shards of pottery, bronze tools and early grain cultivation hint that civilization in Southeast Asia may have developed parallel to, or even before, that in the Middle East and China.

Within the past few years a dig in Thailand uncovered a fragment containing a husk of rice dating (by Carbon-14 processing) to at least 3500 B.C. "This is as much as a thousand years earlier than rice has been dated for either India or China where some archeologists have claimed rice was first domesticated."[4]

Some experts even theorize that neolithic (late Stone Age) culture reached northern China from Southeast Asia—rather than the other way round—about 7000 B.C. Accidental voyages to Taiwan and Japan came perhaps around 4000 B.C. "Sometime during the third millenium B.C., the now expert, boat-using people of Southeast Asia were entering the islands of Indonesia and the Philippines."[5]

This is not the place for a learned discussion of the evidence. The important point: Southeast Asia possessed a sophisticated civilization, about which too little is yet known, before Indian and Chinese cultures began to reshape the region. Thus, some Asians object to terms like Indo-China or even Indonesia because they may "obscure the fact that the areas involved are not mere cultural appendages of India or China but have their own strongly marked individuality."[6]

Southeast Asia possessed significant navigational skills, domesticated animals and complex irrigation for its rice fields *before* the Indian and Chinese periods. Java, for example, had developed the famous *batik* art, *gamelan* orchestras and *wayang* puppet plays still distinctive marks of Indonesian life. Another difference: Indian Hinduism never succeeded in passing on the rigid caste stratification, nor did Indian Islam create the isolation of women so prevalent in much of the Islamic world.

The fragments of history emerging in recent years have been used effectively by national leaders to give the emerging nations a sense of pride in their own uniqueness. Legend, history, and myth have been invoked to fire national imagination. The Burmese recall the golden age of Pa-gan. Resistance to outside domination sustained the Vietnamese against the French. An American visited North Vietnam during the height of American bombing and was struck with how often he was shown relics and memorials of the traditional Vietnamese fight against the Chinese. Cambodians point to Angkor and the Thais find unity in their monarchy.

By the time of Jesus Christ, at least, serious contact existed between Southeast Asian nations and India. Various theories explain how Indian traders, colonists or missionaries arrived in Southeast Asia and began the process of "Indianizing" the various peoples they found. Again, however,

The becak, the Indonesian version of the bicycle rickshaw, is still one of the most popular modes of transportation in Southeast Asian towns. The physical strain of driving the vehicle reduces the life expectancy of drivers to 35.

contemporary scholarship suggests that Southeast Asians may well have made their way to India also. No matter: Indian influence on Southeast Asia has been deep and enduring. Hinduism, Buddhism and Islam all entered Southeast Asia from India. Sanskrit became the Latin of medieval Asia; today the sensuous dances of Thailand, Laos, Cambodia and Indonesia all depict various Hindu legends like the Ramayana. Bali, which remains Hindu, most clearly reflects the complex heritage that India deposited in the region.

The other great cultural stream flowing into Southeast Asia began in China. It went beyond the cultural and religious influence of India to effect intense political and economic changes.

Although most directly felt in Vietnam–ruled by China for about 1,000 years until A.D. 939–journeys by representatives of various Chinese dynasties exacted tribute far and wide in the region.

Today, the flowing Ao-Dai of Vietnamese women obviously comes from the Chinese cheongsam; the Indonesian sarong, on the other hand, originated in India. Burmese men wear a louynygi, developed from the Indian sarong, but a Chinese-style shirt. The Chinese-type plow is employed in Vietnam, the Philippines and North Borneo, but South Borneo, Cambodia and Laos used an Indian-influenced plow.

ONCE-UPON-A-TIME KINGDOMS

Wisps of memory in the form of stoles and fragmentary writings remind the twentieth century of once-great kingdoms in the region.

Funan, rising to power almost 2,000 years ago from a Mekong delta base, stretched eastward through Thailand and down into the Malay peninsula at its zenith. Chinese merchants marveled at Funan's handiwork; some of the gold and bronze artifacts surviving the centuries tantalize with inscriptions of Roman Emperor Antoninus Pius.

Funan fell about the sixth century to an early Khmer empire the Chinese identified as Chen-la. As their territory swelled and the coffers filled, the Khmer kings, forerunners to Cambodia which now calls itself the Khmer Republic, spent centuries constructing the fabled Angkor. For reasons still unclear, the Khmer weakened and probably fell to expanding Siamese might in the early fifteenth century. The Siamese (Thai) kingdom,* during its historical moment, created another glittering city, Ayutthaya, which did not survive the ravages of time. Its ruins near Bangkok do not compare with Pa-gan or Angkor.

A durable empire named Champa sprang up in Central Vietnam about the same time as Funan but endured on the South China Sea for about 1,700 years before dying out as the Vietnamese people emerged. Centered in the ancient city of Hue, the Chams flaunted history as they expired. No one today understands fully how they constructed their remarkably smooth temples, a process of baking the bricks in place, using no mortar.

The great kingdoms were by no means limited to the mainland. Srivijaya, the most powerful of several significant kingdoms of the seventh century on Java and Sumatra in Indonesia, emerged into our knowledge without fanfare and disappeared almost 1,000 years later. Based at Palembang in Sumatra, it clearly controlled the vital Straits of Malacca and Sundra and thus could monitor and tax the trade between India and the Arab world at one pole, China on the other. Its own ships traveled as far as China and India; history shows that both Cambodia and the Philippines were touched, perhaps even dominated for a time, by Srivijaya.

Central Java produced several powerful groups during this period. Reaching its peak in the fourteenth century the most important was another sea-oriented power, the Majapahit. It ranged ever further, making claims to Siam, Cambodia and Annam (central Vietnam).

All of the kingdoms outlined were more or less Buddhist. Certainly the incredible monuments left behind–Borobudur in central Java, Pa-gan and Angkor–were inspired by devotion to the Buddha. And by the end of

*The word Thai is a descriptive term for a language group living in Thailand, Laos, North Vietnam and northern Burma. The country was known as Siam until 1939, Thailand until 1946, Siam until 1949 and Thailand thereafter.

the fifteenth century, Hinduism was almost lost as a practiced religion, although its cultural legacy remains until today.

In 1292 Marco Polo, on his way home from China, stopped off in Sumatra and reported the beginnings of what would otherwise be lost to history: Islamic proselytizing in Southeast Asia. Conversions had begun, the message carried initially by devout traders from Gujerat in India. Slowly Islam began to replace Buddhism in the Malay world, especially after the birth of the city-state, Malacca. Perched on the western coast of the Malay peninsula, inheriting the control in the Straits of Malacca from Srivijaya, Malacca became the most important commercial center in Southeast Asia early in the fifteenth century. It paid tribute to the Chinese emperor in exchange for help against the continuing thrusts of Siam. And, from this center, Islam slowly spread over the region.

ENTER THE EUROPEANS

Malacca was the magnet which attracted European interests to Southeast Asia. After a bloody battle in 1511 Portuguese adventurer Don Alfonso de Albuquerque took Malacca. The Portuguese had a double purpose: to wrest control from the Arabs of trade through the Straits of Malacca to China and the Spice Islands (the Moluccas of Indonesia) and, under urging by Pope Alexander VI, to end Malacca's role as the center of Islamization.

Thus came Europeans bent on loading their boats with the riches of the East and depositing Christianity at the same time. Dennis Bloodworth has commented that Westerners usually think of conversions to Islam in terms of angry Arabs slaying infidels in holy wars.

> In much of the Malay world of Southeast Asia, however, Islam meant the sufi, the emotional yet gentle missionary who sailed through the islands, adapting the sharp edges of his faith to the curves of the cults he found, and reconciling them through their common denominator of medieval mysticism. Christianity, on the other hand, was carried to the East with cutlass and cannon, and if the white men that so unfortunately seemed to go with it were not gratuitously bullying the benighted, they were using any local display of enmity toward their priests as a pretext for laying violent hands upon kings and their countries. In this way the persecution of Christian missionaries by two emperors of Annam lit a powder train of events that ended with Paris writing "French Indochina" across the entire eastern half of the Southeast Asian mainland.[7]

The Portuguese were disappointed not to control completely the spice trade, but they did well enough. Yet their missionary activity, accompanied by a continuing brutality, actually pushed a number of Malay leaders to embrace Islam as a political counter to Portugal.

Later the "gentle missionaries" would arrive. Certainly in part because of the uncharitable beginnings, the growth of the Christian community has always been slow. Most converts to Christianity came from Chinese immigrants, Indian Hindus or animists in the hill tribes. Very few Buddhists and Muslims have converted to Christianity.

Malacca became a Portuguese center in 1511. Ten years later another Portuguese expedition, led by Magellan, sailed by the Spice Islands and bumped into Cebu Island in the Philippines. Magellan found no spices, tried to convert the residents and lost his life for his efforts. Two further Portuguese attempts to get hold of the Philippines failed, and to their dismay they saw the Spanish succeed in Cebu in 1565. Manila, the oldest permanent Western community in Asia, was founded in 1571 by the Spanish–who named the islands for their "most Catholic of Kings," Philip II. Islam had made its way into the Philippines by way of Mindanao and the Sulu Islands, where it remains strong until this day. Had Spain arrived fifty years later, the Philippines today would almost certainly be as strongly Muslim as Indonesia and Malaysia. But the Philippines today is 90 percent Christian, predominantly Roman Catholic.

The Dutch found Southeast Asia about seventy years after the Portuguese took Malacca. Seeking the spice trade through the United East India Company, the Dutch, undercutting Malacca, made Batavia (now Jakarta, Indonesia's capital) the center of activity in the spice trade. The Dutch concentrated on Java for almost two hundred years, but by 1909 the Dutch had absorbed all of what is today Indonesia.

Three Anglo-Burmese wars from 1824 to 1885 dragged Burma into England's Indian empire; by 1826 the British controlled Penang Island, Malacca and Singapore (founded in 1819). Known as the Straits settlements, the three ports gave England control of the Straits of Malacca and led to eventual British dominance of the whole of the Malay peninsula, plus North Borneo.

The French consolidated their hold over Laos, Cambodia and Vietnam during the last half of the nineteenth century. And when in 1896, with the first nationalist revolution in Asia, the Philippines revolted against the Spanish, the United States undercut the attempt to set up an independent state. As a result of the Spanish-American War, the United States annexed the Philippines in 1898 and by 1900 had squelched the rebels. America now had its colony in Asia, even if Washington tried to avoid use of the term.

Thailand's history is different from the rest of the region because it never knew direct colonialization by the Europeans. This was partly because the British and French wanted a buffer between them, and also because of the adroit and perceptive leadership of King Mongkut (1851-1868)–whose mischaracterization in *The King and I* so offends Thais that the movie has never been shown publicly in Thailand–and his son, King Chulalongkorn (1868-1910). Aware that Thailand could not resist the European power directly, the kings made concessions where necessary, many of them painful. The main loss: four states to England on the Malay peninsula (still part of Malaysia) and several Lao and Cambodian provinces to France.

Clearly the European era had an enormous impact on the culture, politics, society and economy of Asia. Christianity was added to the region, claiming the loyalty of a small but influential percentage of people. Southeast Asia's orientation toward China and India changed abruptly. Boundary lines were drawn arbitrarily, according to the vagaries of colonial power. Whole communities were split as lines slashed through natural groupings: a sizeable Khmer population cut off from Cambodia by the French definition of Cochin China in Vietnam; a unified Laotian Thai "family" sundered by the new Thai-Laotian border; Malaysia and Indonesia separate states primarily because the Dutch ruled one place, the British the other. Generations of natives had no opportunity to administer their own forms of government.

The most detrimental and probably longest lasting result of the European period involved the economy. Europeans were there to exploit the wealth of the region, to maximize their profits. The way Southeast Asia's economics were developed had everything to do with the needs in London, Paris, the Hague, but nothing with planned growth in the colonies. "... the underdevelopment of Southeast Asia was the price it had to pay for the development of the affluent nations of the West; the workings of the colonial system resulted in a steady transfer of wealth from the colonial dependencies to the metropolitan country."[8]

Also created during the colonial era were local economic elites who learned to feather their own nests by cooperating with the foreign interests against their own countries. Using power built up over generations, some of those families continue to thwart true national economic development.

The colonial period also contributed to the population pressures still with Asia. For example, the cultivation methods of the Dutch on Java called for heavy concentrations of people in one place. Attempts now by the Indonesian government to entice people from overpopulated Java back to the outer islands have been unsuccessful.

THE OVERSEAS CHINESE

The always strong Chinese influence in the region was intensified in the past one hundred years as a new wave from China's overloaded Southeast Coast moved into Southeast Asia. While some came as established traders to commercial centers like Bangkok or Jakarta and others settled in remote, thinly-populated areas such as Borneo, the most obvious attraction came from work as indentured laborers in the tin mines and rubber plantations of, say, Malaysia. The British also encouraged them

Queenstown is the first satellite housing area to be built in Singapore. Built between 1960 and 1965, it houses 150,000 people. Similar housing now exists in Hong Kong and Kuala Lumpur and is planned for Manila and Jakarta.

to come as coolies on the docks of Singapore and Penang. Hard working, determined and thrifty, the Chinese moved quickly upward on the economic ladder. From peddlers to shopkeepers, rickshaw drivers to truck owners, coolies to ship owners, pawnbrokers to bankers, the Chinese made a tremendous impact and contribution to the region. Yet as a group midway between the local peasant and the Western colonialists or the native elites, their economic power made them conspicuous, envied and from time to time targets. An example: two centuries as managers and middle people for the Dutch led about three million Chinese, by some estimates, to control two-thirds of Indonesia's trade when independence arrived.

Numbering perhaps twenty million, they form an internal market force within Southeast Asia. Families and clans finance each other around the region, often from Chinese banks in Hong Kong and Singapore. Proud of their culture, strong in their linguistic and family ties, quietly scorning their less aggressive fellow citizens, the Chinese are not going to be assimilated any time soon into Southeast Asia. This is especially true in the Islamic world, where intermarriage demands that the Chinese convert to Islam. Among many objections, the Chinese refuse to give up pork, essential to some of the most sumptuous Chinese cuisine.

The colonial period brought a new respect for justice, broader understanding of administration and an enforced period of peace among the nations of this tropical littoral. And, ironically, the educational systems of the West introduced political concepts that undermined colonial theory. The most western of Asian states, the Philippines, constructed the first nationalist movement. They knew about the American revolution. Vietnamese drank deeply of the French revolution in Paris. In England, Malays learned that England "never did, nor never shall, lie at the proud foot of conqueror."

THE JAPANESE LESSON

Just as nationalist feeling was building, the whole rotten system collapsed in December, 1941. With stunning swiftness the Japanese landed on the Malay peninsula the same day they bombed Pearl Harbor. Three months later Japan controlled Malaya, Singapore, Indonesia, the Philippines and Hong Kong, as well as earlier gained Indochina, and had access to Thailand as Bangkok continued to compromise with the inevitable. The Japanese were in Burma, driving toward India.

The Japanese occupation of Southeast Asia was marked by a brutality not forgotten or forgiven by most Asians. But the Europeans had been humbled. A story is told of the shocked reaction in Singapore's Cricket Club when the British ships, *Repulse* and *Prince of Wales,* were bombed to the bottom of the South China Sea. Not a word was spoken; then a glass, dropped from the hand of a shocked Englishman, shattered the silence. Singapore, the "impregnable fortress," collapsed in ignominy. In Indonesia, the Japanese built an army of natives to defend against allied counterattack. After the war, these troops became the armies of liberation against the Dutch.

INDEPENDENCE: RHETORIC AND REALITY

The postwar era was marked by the heady prospect of independence. By 1949 Burma, the Philippines and Indonesia had achieved *"merdeka,"* independence. The French persisted in Indochina until Dien Bien Phu scrambled the empire. The Geneva Conference in 1954 brought independence to Cambodia, Laos and a split Vietnam, calling for elections there to unify the country in 1956. That they never came is part of the tragedy of Vietnam. Even Malaya, where independence arrived more slowly to the racially complex nation, became independent in 1957. In 1963 Malaya metamorphosed into Malaysia, the awkward joining of Malaya, Singapore and the North Borneo territories of Britain. Singapore, with its large Chinese majority, was pushed out of Malaysia in 1965 and has since been an independent state linking its fate largely with Western economic interests.

Reading–not incorrectly–the creation of Malaysia as the continued working of the long British hand, Indonesia's charismatic, if shortsighted, President Sukarno set into motion a policy of confrontation which created serious disorder in the region and economic chaos at home.

Political instability had accompanied the coming of independence. The Indonesians fought the Dutch for four years before they finally surrendered their claim to the beloved East Indies in 1949. And not until 1963 did the Dutch finally give up on the western half of New Guinea, now known as Irian Jaya.

Not least of the ironies at the end of the colonial period involved the weapons used either to resist it or to fight against the "safe" regimes often established for the turnover of power. In the Philippines the Americans had provided the Hukbalahaps with weapons to fight the Japanese, as they had the "Free Thais" in Thailand and the Vietminh in Vietnam. The British did likewise for the Thakins in Burma and the People's Anti-Japanese Army in Malaya. By 1949 all these groups were fighting against their governments, some as Communists and some as nationalists. A further irony: in some cases the Western forces supported national leaders who had collaborated with the Japanese.

Gradually the rebellions ran down, although it took the British and Malays until 1960 to lock up the Malay insurgency. And, of course, the combination of nationalists and Communists determined to reunite Vietnam fight on until this day.

Attempts at regional cooperation for defense and economic development continued to bump into barriers in the relations between nations. The Philippines made a shaky claim to Malaysia's state of Sabah on the northeast tip of Borneo in the late 1960's, exacerbating relations between those two nations. The almost sibling rivalry between giant Indonesia and small but economically promising Malaysia overcame confrontation after the fall of Sukarno in 1965. But the events surrounding his fall–an attempted coup by Communist forces resulting in a bloodbath of retribution by Indonesians against their Chinese fellow countrymen–still haunt the nation. And tensions yet exist between Indonesia and Malaysia along the Borneo border as they do between Thailand and Malaysia on their borders: the four southernmost states of Thailand are predominantly Muslim with natural affinities to Malaysia. The remnant of the 1950's insurgency occasionally surfaces to blast a building or kill a few Malaysians from a base across the border in Thailand.

Still, the shared struggle to become independent usually links the region, outside bloody Indochina, in a kinship which allows more cooperation than disagreement.

FROM POLITICS TO ECONOMICS

Having shed direct colonial rule, the nations of Southeast Asia entered the new period full of hope and determination. For decades the driving force in the region had been political: freedom, *merdeka*, and independence moved people and nations.

But the internally unbalanced societies and the strong economic ties to foreign centers of trade seemed to undercut much of the Asian possibility. Early promise seemed to fade. "By the end of the 1960's, despite what had been accomplished in some spheres and despite that vast potential for development that remained, the mood of Southeast Asia was one of hesitation, of trepidation and of more caution, rather than creativity and boldness. Hope and experimentation had not been abandoned, but a gnawing sense of crisis, of irresolution and frustration had cast a pall over progress. In the spring of 1966 Sinnathamby Rajaratnam (Singapore's foreign minister) posed the question, "What has gone wrong with the Asian revolution? Why has it not been able to fulfill the great things people expected of it?"[9]

While speaking to the Christian Conference of Asia in 1973 Dr. M. M. Thomas, director of the Christian Institute for the Study of Religion and Society in Bangalore, India, said that nationalism–the earlier political drive for national identity–did not provide the lever necessary to bring real social justice to Asia because "nationalism has become confined to the elite, and in too many nations of Asia, as an ideology for their own search for power and conspicuous consumption." He added that in many countries the emphasis on "national security, unity and stability tends to become an ethos for preserving the existing structure against change and to justify the suppression of democratic rights and mass action for change."[10]

For the past two decades the serious concern for those looking for social justice in Southeast Asia has moved into the economic realm. In his essay on Malaysia Lim Mah Hui demonstrates how the bottom 20 percent of the Malaysians share only 4 percent of the national income.

Dr. Thomas was speaking generally. But an example of his point might be the Philippines. Ferdinand Marcos, nearing the end of his presidency under the constitution, placed the Philippines under martial law in September, 1972. Many outside observers have said that the drastic curtailment of democratic processes was necessary for national development. The American Chamber of Commerce in Manila wired Marcos its congratulations.

In September, 1973, the *New York Times* reported that Gerardo Sicat, "the usually cautious director of the national development authority, foresees a possible 10 percent economic growth this year and says, 'Our country has the makings of a new economic miracle in Asia.'

"The optimistic outlook is attributed to great social stability under martial law, a large balance-of-payments surplus resulting from high world commodity prices and increased domestic and foreign investment stemming from more favorable regulations and government attitudes."[11]

Some Balinese women who live in villages off the tourist paths continue to do their daily chores in traditional topless dress.

But in October, 1973, a survey of 154 Roman Catholics–including 14 Bishops, 59 priests and 22 sisters–in all parts of the Philippines challenged that conventional wisdom. "Seventy-five percent of all respondents feel that the political situation throughout the country is worse now than it was before martial law." Prices were described as having risen drastically; "in quantitative terms, they were said to have doubled, tripled or quadrupled since Martial Law."

The survey told of growing unemployment and widescale avoidance of the national minimum wage of 7 Pesos (about $1.03) per day. "Many stevedores receive only 3 (Pesos) per day, logging workers are sometimes not paid for from four to eight months, and male sugar workers in Negros receive as low as 1.50 per day; women 1.00; and children 0.75. . . . Tobacco workers in Isabela and La Union receive as low as 2.00 and 3.00 per day. . . . Among logging, sugar and tobacco workers the *cantina* system is in operation. *Cantinas* on the average charge 30 percent more per item than do ordinary stores. Laborers generally must buy from the *cantinas.*"[12]

It would appear that the Philippines' economic miracle does not promise to redress the economic imbalance. The poorest people in the Philippines work on the sugar plantations; the richest people in the Philippines own those plantations.

Asia's basic problem as told by Singapore's Finance Minister Goh Keng Swee to the same Christian Conference of Asia meeting addressed by Thomas, is poverty, "poverty so abject that only those who have seen for themselves the human degradation which poverty brings have a true picture of the situation. But poverty in the poor regions of Asia is different from that of poverty as it is known in the West. For instance, recently I read in an American newspaper bitter complaints that, as a result of inflation, the poor in the United States can only afford hamburgers and not steaks. In Asia, the poor live permanently on the borderline of starvation."[13]

Many subjects concern Southeast Asia today. The nations of the region, with Malaysia taking the first formal steps in mid-1974, will once again have diplomatic relations with China. Japan's overpowering economic presence in the region causes deep concern and occasional demonstrations, such as those following Japan's Prime Minister Kakuei Tanaka around the region in early 1974. The heavy American political, economic and military presence is another international issue. Any naive talk about the post-Indochina war period is cut off in this region by the knowledge Southeast Asians have that in Cambodia and Vietnam there is no peace. Regional cooperation has increased, if slowly, through a non-military grouping called the Association of Southeast Asian Nations (ASEAN) involving Indonesia, the Philippines, Thailand, Malaysia and Singapore, with Burma a frequent visitor at meetings. Some critics see ASEAN as an instrument making foreign exploitation of area resources easier. At any rate, some debate–at least internally–takes place on the pros and cons of foreign investment and the power of multinational corporations.

But the big issue for the 1970's remains the poverty that grips so large a part of Southeast Asia. That theme is played back in various ways in a number of the essays in this book

THE PLACES

The Southeast Asia addressed as a geographical unit in this book is in fact composed of quite diverse peoples and cultures.

External events often have differing impacts on the region's nations. The quadrupling of oil prices in 1973 hit most of Asia with devastating force. Diverse development plans for Southeast Asian states all require oil and natural gas consumption, essential to industrial growth and food production, at a rate of increase higher than the industrialized nations. These paper plans were blasted in most of Southeast Asia by the quantum leap in the costs of oil and petroleum products.

But to Indonesia, exporting over one million barrels of oil a day, the higher prices meant much higher earnings from oil sales. Malaysia also produces more oil than it consumes; Burma finds part of its requirements on its own territory. Clearly the problem was viewed differently for these nations than it was in the Philippines, or Thailand, or Vietnam which import all of their petroleum needs.

The pressures of limited food supplies will also be felt with greater intensity in overcrowded Java, for example, than in Malaysia with its much smaller population.

In this section one specific issue concerning a Southeast Asian nation is addressed by an Asian writer. While the subject may be of interest to all of Southeast Asia, not all countries experience the same concern. The Philippines, long known for its open public debate and clamorous politics, suddenly found in September, 1972, that martial law had throttled public discourse long taken for granted. After the problems of martial law are discussed by Senator Jovite Salonga, Sulak Sivaraksa presents the Thai move away from military dictatorship and contradictions within that development.

Burma has taken yet another approach to national development, a closing of its doors to outsiders and a consolidation of national identity. U

Kyaw Than analyzes the Burmese experiment, not very well understood by outsiders.

Malaysia has two great advantages in contemporary Asia: a small population and abundant natural resources. Yet its development has been hindered by internal tensions between a politically predominant Malay community and an economically potent ethnic Chinese population almost as large as the Malays. Lim Mah Hui argues racial conflicts will remain as long as the majority of the Malays, Chinese and Indians living in Malaysia see their economic plight in racial terms.

"Women in Southeast Asia find themselves in an ambivalent position. On the one hand their active participation in economic and social life in a time of rapid change is sought and urgently needed; on the other hand it is subject in practice to limitations and discriminations."[14] Tue Hien Morrow discusses how women in Vietnam have endured a long history of war and dislocation.

Finally in this section Joseph Lelyveld outlines the continuing deep involvement of the United States in the region. The United States, of the three most important outside influences on the region, alone includes economic, political and military presence. Japan's economic influence is increasingly great in Southeast Asia; the cultural and indirect political influence of China casts a long shadow.

THE PHILIPPINES UNDER MARTIAL LAW

Senator Jovite Salonga

In September, 1972, having almost completed seven of his eight-year term under a Constitution that rules out reelection, President Ferdinand E. Marcos proclaimed martial law, saying that the nation was faced by an emergency "amounting to an actual state of war" between the Republic and the Communists and other armed groups.

It cannot be denied that before martial law there were many bombing

---

Senator Jovite Salonga was, before martial law abolished the Philippine Senate, the only Protestant in the Senate and one of the most vocal opponents to President Ferdinand E. Marcos's government. His opposition to martial law, imposed in 1972, continues in many public and private ways. The 53-year-old former dean of the Law School in Manila's Far Eastern University was severely injured in a grenade attack in August, 1971, at a rally of his opposition Liberal Party.

incidents, whose origins are none too clear up to now. It cannot be denied that there were private armies that should never have been allowed to exist and multiply in the first place. It cannot be denied that the press was sometimes licentious and irresponsible. It cannot be denied that there was much graft and many politicians and public officials who engaged in corrupt activities. It cannot be denied that the bulk of the nation's wealth was in the hands of a privileged few.

But an increasing number of Filipinos today question whether martial law was and is the proper remedy, whether it could possibly be worse than the disease, and whether in the long run it may not bring about the very instability it was meant to prevent.

For the sake of peace and order, political dissent was proscribed and freedom of speech and press, freedom of peaceful assembly and all kinds of mass action, including labor strikes and picketing, were curtailed. Mass media were shut down for a time, with only a few allowed to operate under strict censorship. For the sake of the New Society, Congress was locked up and the Judiciary was placed under the control of the President, who assumed all powers of government. Political activity was prohibited and important political leaders and public opinion molders were either imprisoned or discredited. Political and legislative processes were denigrated.

Yet the President was able to justify his so-called "constitutional authoritarian" government by virtue of an alleged *consultation* with hurriedly organized Citizens' Assemblies, held in January, 1973. The "ratification" he proclaimed for the New Constitution was promptly challenged in the Supreme Court, a majority of whom said that it had not been validly ratified. In a masterpiece of *non sequitur,* the Court ruled, however, that there was "no more judicial obstacle to considering it in force." The Chief Justice withdrew from the Court, new Justices were appointed and both the old and new Justices were required to take the oath to defend the New Constitution. The consultation, sometimes called "plebiscite," was considered by many as a farce.

President Marcos is right when he speaks of the need for economic equality and a better distribution of wealth. But the disturbing fact is that we now witness bigger concentrations of wealth and power, not only in the hands of a few Filipino oligarchs (only some Filipino oligarchs were put out of business) but in the hands of vast American and Japanese multinational companies. How rhetoric can be matched by reality is one of the biggest problems under martial law.

It is now fashionable to speak of foreign investments, foreign capital and technology, foreign loans and foreign aid. We are told foreign investors are all competing with one another to be here, and that we should welcome them with open arms. Up to a certain point this may be good, in that they provide jobs. But the basic question is whether these will lift our people or whether they will enrich only a few and aggravate the poverty of the many, thus perpetuating our underdevelopment.

Ironically, the situation today is worse than immediately before martial law. Muslim rebels are up in arms in Mindanao, and the controlled press speaks of clashes in some parts of Visayas and Luzon. There is more criminality than before. Salaries and wages are very low, but prices are sky-high. Beauty contests and international exhibitions, while amusing the people, only serve to dramatize the thoughtless extravagance of the privileged few and the irrational sense of priorities. Graft is rampant. "Backsliding" is the favorite term used by the policy-makers in condemning corruption and influence peddling.

The next few years will be very critical in the life of this country. The economy will be subjected to very severe strains because of the oil squeeze, the galloping inflation causing alarming increases in the prices of almost all commodities, probable shortages of basic items and worsening unemployment. The typical Filipino can stand loss of freedom of speech and press as long as he and his family are not hungry; it will be a different story altogether if he is out of work and his children begin to cry for food that he cannot afford to give.

The most repressive measures may be resorted to in order to prevent an upheaval. The key factors in such a situation would be the armed forces, the United States government, the awakened masses, the students, the intellectuals and the church.

The United States government has maintained an ambiguous position. Though it extends economic and military aid to the regime, it purports to be neutral, an attitude reminiscent of the policy of neutral intervention several years before it was drawn into the Second World War. The record of the United States in supporting dictatorship in Asia, while preaching democracy everywhere, has diminished its credibility.

The presence of American military bases on Philippine soil is a constant source of irritation. The Philippines cannot claim independence as long as they are here. Nor can some American businessmen and officials pretend they are not intervening in Philippine affairs. The presence of the bases here, plus the military and economic assistance extended to the government, compounded by the reality of tremendous American economic power, render the pretension a mockery. Before martial law, about 80 percent of foreign investments were controlled by American multinational corporations.

Because of American occupation of the Philippines for almost half a century and the repeated avowals of responsible American officials on behalf of individual liberty and democracy, the prestige and credibility of the United States are at stake here more than in any other part of Asia. What happens in the Philippines today will have a great bearing on the credibility of the American government in many Asian countries.

Because of improved peace and order, trade and tourism have picked up, and foreign investors have been attracted by an open-door policy. American businessmen and foreign investors have never had it so good. Low wages, the ban against strikes and mass action, plus a host of incentives and inducements, make some Filipinos wonder if this is still their country.

Student protests, demonstrations, legislative inquiries and nationalistic rulings from the courts have been taken care of by martial law. That explains why the American Chamber of Commerce here supports martial law.

American business firms still dominate key sectors of our economy, but the Japanese are fast catching up and even surpassing them in some areas. The "ratification" of the Philippine-Japanese Treaty of Amity, Commerce and Navigation by President Marcos was done quietly after the Philippine Senate refused to ratify it for twelve years. Up until now the text of the Treaty has not been published in the newspapers. Japanese investments in the first quarter of 1974 exceeded American investments.

The students, particularly in the Manila area, have been laying low for some time. They are under tight surveillance. Idealistic, they have a sharpened sense of injustice. Without any vested interest to promote, they are credible. They come from all classes, and it may be difficult to strike them down so easily. The well-known student leaders in 1970 and 1971 are either in army camps or have gone underground. The identity and caliber of the new leaders are not yet known.

The intellectuals, by and large, have suffered from the regime and, because of its excesses and contradictions, are resentful. Those who are in the employ of the present regime are either technocrats or propagandists.

The church in the Philippines, with a Christian constituency estimated to exceed 90 percent of the total population, can be a decisive factor.

The major religious superiors of the Catholic church–which counts about 80 percent of the population in its membership–conducted a national survey in November of 1973, over a year after the declaration of martial law. The report catalogued the situation of land reform, labor conditions, politics, squatters, prices, mass media and the role of the church. The government's claim to progress in land reform, considered to be the most important feature of the New Society, was squarely disputed by the report, which painted a generally dismal picture of the Philippine society under martial law. Although the report concluded that the Catholic church was "seen as going along with the present situation in spite of oppressions and injustice, with no plan of action, no clear stand," there were definite progressive elements in the church whose prophetic ministry and leadership are outstanding. Sixteen bishops sent a letter to President Marcos immediately after the declaration of martial law

Cutting sugar cane in the Philippines. In the Philippines the richest families in the nation own the sugar fields, the poorest families harvest the sugar.

requesting that it be ended as soon as possible, that detainees be dealt with fairly in civil courts and that basic freedoms of speech and press be restored to the citizenry. Priests, nuns and lay leaders who continued to push for these things were put behind bars or face deportation proceedings, but many have been released. On August 27, 1974, the Sacred Heart Novitiate in Novaliches, Quezon City, was raided. Priests, nuns and lay persons were subjected to humiliating treatment, and 21 were placed under arrest, including an activist priest. The mass media reported that the raid was carried out with the knowledge and assistance of the Catholic church hierarchy–a false representation which Archbishop Jaime Sin of Manila and Father Provincial Benigno Mayo, S.J., promptly exposed and condemned. The embarrassed authorities released most of those arrested and affirmed the rule that no church or religious institution shall be raided without the previous consent of its head. A few days later, the Catholic Bishops delivered a letter to the President unanimously asking for the gradual lifting of martial law and the restoration of basic civil liberties.

Of the Protestant churches, the most important are the United Church of Christ in the Philippines, the Methodists, the Baptists, the Lutherans, the Episcopalians, the Iemelif (Evangelical Methodist Church) and the Iglesia Evangelica Unida de Cristo. Soon after martial law was imposed, the heads of these churches, along with the head of the Philippine Independent Church, expressed their support to the President "for his efforts to stop lawlessness and the machinations of those who would destroy our Government and deprive our peiple of their dignity and freedom."

In December, 1973, however, the National Council of Churches of the Philippines passed two important resolutions: (1) a resolution requesting the President to lift martial law, except in such areas where the constitutional grounds for their continuance may still exist, and (2) a resolution asking the President to restore freedom of speech and freedom of the press, even if he does not lift martial law.

These resolutions were passed after a group of young Protestant ministers, concerned about the message of the Gospel for our people in these trying times, made an analysis of present-day conditions. They saw the gap between official propaganda and reality and felt it was part of their prophetic ministry to proclaim the truth, regardless of consequences. These ministers signed a Manifesto which reviewed the events since the imposition of martial law, recounting the pronouncements of the President to the effect that there was "no more emergency," that "the Communist apparatus has been dismantled," that there has been a "big leap in the economy" and that martial law should "not be made a permanent institution in our national life." Together they drafted the following:

> The discipline of a command society has unfortunately bred fear and mutual suspicion. Laborers and wage earners dare not press for higher wages and better working conditions through concerted action for fear that they might be dismissed. Common citizens, told to appear in military quarters to answer complaints that should have been presented in civil courts since they only involve family affairs or disputes regarding private property or contractual obligations, shudder in fear of being detained. Worse, people are afraid to talk candidly about their public officials, even in whispers. People are disheartened to ventilate their feelings about their government for fear that their neighbors or associates might report them to the military authorities. People are reluctant to assemble and speak of common grievances for fear that they might be brought to the nearest army stockade. When they read their newspapers or sit before their tv or radio sets, they know what kind of news and comment they will get; a one-sided presentation and a chorus of unanimous praise for their high officials. They know it is the organized system of coercion and fear that brought this about.

In one year's time, at the prodding of young ministers, the atmosphere in the National Council of Churches underwent a tremendous change. But on June 27, 1974, the NCCP Headquarters was raided, the General Secretary was arrested, along with three foreign missionaries and Filipino staff members. Most of them have been released. The American missionaries were required to leave. The NCCP hierarchy did not make a public stand.

But the concerned ministers of the various Protestant groups continue to discharge their prophetic ministry, despite the risks and the many difficulties confronting them. These ministers, knowing the severe restrictions of martial law on the basic liberties of individuals and knowing how often the churches give up their ministry by conveniently aligning themselves with those in power, continue to proclaim the truth, defend basic human rights and fight for a society that is not only orderly, but free and just. There could be more of them, but some ministers find "peace and order" more important than the basic human values of justice, truth and freedom. They are attracted by the propaganda of discipline, apparently forgetting that discipline without justice is the very essence of oppression. Others are afraid that their involvement might divide the church, and that it is better to be "spiritual" and engage in abstract discourses on justice and love in order to preserve unity. But unity based on compromise with injustice and evasion of duty is a sham. Many lay persons hope that the church, its ministers and leaders, will not be afraid to continue speaking out against society's evils and injustices. Sometimes, these ministers and leaders doubt whether what they do will make any difference, considering the risks they take. But they know that one man standing up for what is good and right can, in God's own season, make a real difference. For history tells them that a handful of people who know what they believe and are not afraid to say it and die for it, if necessary, can change the world.

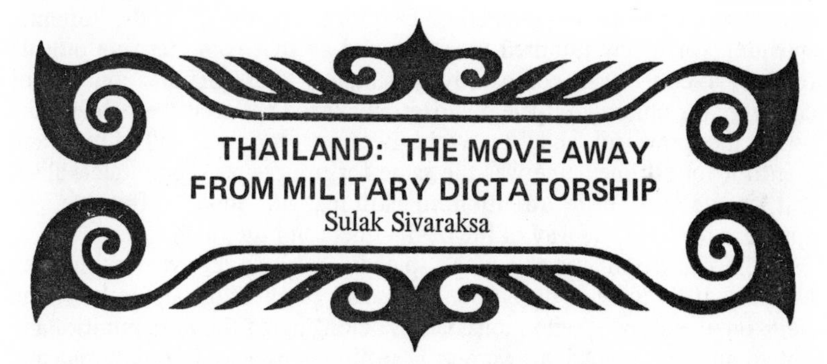

THAILAND: THE MOVE AWAY FROM MILITARY DICTATORSHIP

Sulak Sivaraksa

When the military government of Field Marshal Thanom Kittikachorn collapsed with stunning swiftness in October, 1973, a surprised world

---

A special lecturer in philosophy at Chulalongkorn and Thammasat universities in Bangkok, Sulak Sivaraksa has edited several magazines, written seven books, and holds legal credentials as a barrister-at-law at the Middle Temple, London. Among his books are *My Life as an Editor* and *Biographies of Buddhist Monks.* He has been an editorial advisor to *Solidarity* and is a member of the International Press Institute, International Association of Cultural Freedom and International House.

watched as Thailand began to take on what seemed like a new political shape.

A nation long known for its absolute monarchies and, since 1932 its military dictatorships, appeared to be going against the grain. At a time when some observers said that authoritarian governments were desired by Asians, in Thailand the move seemed to be toward more representative and constitutional government.

Demonstrations of thousands of students in Bangkok had been bloodied by heavy military gunfire; hundreds died, thousands were wounded. But the students came to be for a time the symbol of a nation's discontent with corrupt leadership; tens of thousands more students gathered in Bangkok. Suddenly, Thanom, deputy prime minister Prapas Charusathiara, and Thanom's unpopular son, Colonel Narong Kittikachorn, were out; King Bhumibol Adulyadej named the Rector of Thammasat University, Sanya Dharmasakti, 66, the first civilian prime minister since 1957. Thanom, Prapas and Narong–now called Thailand's "three most hated men"–fled the country.

Did the events of 1973 indeed mean that the Thai people, so long cut off from voice in their nation's politics, would at last have a democratic and representative political system?

To address this fundamental question, we need to look back to old Siam. It has been said that to understand the present and predict the future, we should know our past. In days of old, the Kingdom of Siam was known as an "absolute monarchy." Despite the myths about the "oriental splendor" of a few hundred years ago and all that connotes, life outside the royal court was comparatively simple. Although the concept of equality was unknown, little polarization existed between the rich and the poor, the powerful and the weak. Because food was still simple and plentiful for all, medicine was the same for princes and commoners alike, and people paid little attention to clothing, not much difference was apparent between the way of life of the rulers and the ruled.

The exception was the king's splendid palaces; yet even within such buildings little interior decoration was seen. People, high and low, sat and slept on the floor. Some monasteries, belonging to the communities and not to any one individual, were as beautiful as palaces. Certainly rich and poor people existed, but money was not the main motive in life. Those with wealth concentrated on looking after their people, animals and environment rather than exploiting them to get richer and thus more powerful.

In Siamese society social mobility remained fluid. A daughter of a commoner could become queen overnight. The king's descendants returned to common status after a few generations. Polygamy bridged the gap between nobility and the commoner. A bright village boy could realize importance as a monk; if he desired to leave the holy order, he could become a nobleman. Indeed, in a few instances former monks even became kings.

The majority of the population lived far away from the capital, where central authority hardly ever reached them and money was not very useful. Each village was self-contained, with its own food, shelter and basic resources for a livelihood. Thus the majority of the population knew little about riches and power.

Buddhism exerted its influence on the rich and powerful, whose money and power normally did not extend beyond the big cities. Buddhism counseled against attraction to worldly gains. If the king exercised his might against the cardinal teachings of the Buddha, his rivals would have cause to remove him from the throne.

Buddhism played an equally crucial role in the lives of the majority of the people. Each village usually had a *wat* (monastery) where the abbot was the spiritual as well as civic leader. The *wat* played many roles: school, hospital, community hall, cultural center, art gallery, museum. Whatever the village needed and possessed could be found in the monastery.

The monks, entirely supported by the villagers, would always counsel self-sufficiency and denounce greed for more wealth and power. Yet they also urged love for each other. So the villagers usually helped each other plowing and harvesting, often accompanied by song and dance. Medicine made in the home and monastery was distributed free. Gay ceremonies accompanied the building of a new house, a wedding or even a funeral. Work and play went together. If anything was not done with *sanuk* (enjoying oneself), life was not worth living. Although most people were poor, and life expectancy was short, life was lived with *sanuk* and the people did not feel oppressed.

The ancient monarchical regimes seemed to have had little impact, positive or negative, on the people, except in time of war or great famine. In war they had to suffer the national fate; during famine sometimes the benevolence of the rulers muted the consequences. Nature smiled on the Siamese. The land was not overcrowded; if one place became unsuitable for cultivation, it was simple to emigrate to new areas.

THE COLONIAL IMPACT

Colonial expansion in the nineteenth century began the process of change in Thailand. In order to survive as an independent country, we had to adapt to the Western systems. The tactics of our kings (especially Ramas IV and V, also known as Mongkut and Chulalongkorn) prevented our country from becoming a colony of a foreign power, but it did involve a partial loss of national integrity when the great powers, Britain and France, acquired parts of our territory.

At the same time, Thailand was opened to other Western powers, and legations were established in those countries to make certain they recognized us as a sovereign nation. Our students went abroad to study Western techniques, and some foreign advisers came to Siam in order to adapt our political and social system to suit what was then required for a "civilized" way of life. The result was a reorganized internal administration, the introduction of Western economic, legal and educational systems and the development of electrical grids, railway systems, automobiles and telecommunications. Yet the political base of power remained limited to the king and his court.

The new era brought easy accessibility between king and commoners. No conflict resulted as long as the king was just–as was Rama V (Chulalongkorn, who ruled from 1868-1910)–and was perceived to be running the country for the benefit of the people. But if kings failed to do this, as with Rama VI and VII, people with modern political ideas from their new educational perspectives would criticize them.

In 1932 this new Western educated elite successfully took "absolute power" from the king, although the majority of the people were still not involved in political concerns. From 1932 this country has been known as a "democratic" nation. Although the name of the country changed back and forth between Siam and Thailand, little real change occurred in the political or social structures. The king no longer presided over the government, but the political base of power never included the majority of people.

Since 1932 our governments have always declared themselves democratic, but we were generally ruled by dictatorships of one kind or another. From 1932 to 1974 eleven general elections took place, although real power had never been in the General Assembly. Rather, a small group of people who controlled the armed forces reserved the real power for themselves. When a conflict arose among those contending for the position of Prime Minister, this small group decided. If a peaceful decision was impossible, a *coup d'etat* resulted. Thailand experienced twelve successful and unsuccessful *coups* between 1932 and 1974.

For fifteen years the ruling elite consisted of key civilians as well as naval and military officers. But from 1947 on the military monopolized the power group. Except for two very brief civilian interludes, the Prime Minister has also been *ipso facto* field marshal and supreme commander of the armed forces.

The new elite were in a position to strongly criticize the old "absolute" regimes of "feudalism," yet once in command the new power figures soon saw themselves as the new nobility. Although some of those who wielded power meant well for the country, on the whole they looked down on the common people. And, as they began to acquire wealth and to live in a Western and princely style, corruption crept in.

The association of government ministers and businessmen broadened the corruption. Accompanying the increased cost of living since World War

Thai woman crosses wall circling the squatter section of Dindaeng in Bangkok to obtain water. Inside the wall, constructed by the Municipal authorities to pressure 600 families, no facilities exist. The squatter families are being aided by the Voluntary Movement for People's Organization in Thailand (VOMPORT).

II, many high-ranking officials are known to have acquired wealth by illegitimate means.

Then came the age of United States aid and so-called development help, which meant in effect that money was easily available to "buy" people in authority and tie them to the Western bloc. Thus Thailand, proud of resisting colonialism, found itself led into a neocolonial period, a time when it let American air bases be established all over Siam.

The Japanese have flooded the country in the past two decades also, buying up economic influence and establishing deep roots in the economy, but, unlike the Americans, not involving themselves in Thai politics. People who resisted this national sellout to the neocolonialists were labeled Communists, or Communist sympathizers, and ostracized or put in prison.

The government of Field Marshal Sarit Thanarat used the Communist bogeyman to declare marshal law in 1958, and the country was for a decade without a parliament of elected representatives. The press was not free; the educational system directed itself essentially to training civil servants who could serve the government, technocrats who cared nothing about social justice. The slogan of the period: "Government of the people, by those who know how to operate it for the people." And the prime minister often defended his actions by declaring: "I alone am responsible for the nation."

DEVELOPMENT: THE RICH GROW RICHER

In this political atmosphere, little criticism was heard when national leaders and some international agencies proclaimed that Thailand's national development looked good–the gross national product *was* increasing at a regular rate. But they did not also add that the rich grew richer. New road systems to areas far from Bangkok? That may look good on paper but it made those areas more accessible to Bangkok bureaucrats and businessmen who went upcountry to purchase land. About 85 percent of our population were land-owning farmers, an unusually large number for Southeast Asia. But now more and more became landless. Forestry, mining and agricultural areas, as well as the fishing industry, came more and more to be exploited by few at the expense of the many.

A huge proportion of the government's expenditures occurred in Bangkok to the neglect of rural areas. And when now landless country folk fled to urban Bangkok to seek jobs, they ended up in slum areas and tightly packed squatter zones. Patriots who resisted this exploitation were labeled subversives; so-called Communists in many areas were simply angry Thais who fought against this loss of their traditional way of life.

While people increasingly felt the whole system was excessively corrupt, enriching the people who ran the government, the government itself went through the motions of granting a Constitution in 1968 and holding another general election in early 1969. Not that any risk was involved: the ruling elite appointed the Upper House of Parliament and the majority of the Lower House. Yet even this token representation made them uneasy, so in November, 1971 they dissolved Parliament and annulled the Constitution.

One of the problems facing any despotic government is the line of succession. Field Marshal (and Prime Minister) Thanom hoped to assure the continuation of his clique which had been in power since 1957 by pushing his son, Narong, as his successor. Narong married the daughter of General (and Deputy Prime Minister) Prapas.

But they made a mistake. By pushing Colonel Narong too far too quickly they upset the strong seniority system in the Thai Army. Narong didn't help the plan with greedy, rude and stupid actions. (He once told newspaper interviewers that other than his father the men he most admired in public life were General Franco of Spain, President Park Chung Hee of South Korea and the Shah of Iran.) Narong's unlimited demands for wealth and power upset the "tea money" system of corruption working so effectively for the bureaucrats and businessmen. The anger of the masses was one thing; but such actions made Narong, his father and father-in-law unpopular now within the ruling group.

OCTOBER, 1973: DID ANYTHING REALLY CHANGE?

During the October, 1973 events it appeared that the students and people managed to bring down the corrupt Thanom government. In fact it

An October 13, 1973 demonstration by thousands of Thai students carrying Buddhist flag and pictures of the King. The next day brought "bloody Sunday" when police and military fired wildly into the demonstrators, leading to the fall of the dictatorial government of Thanom Kittikachorn.

was the king and the army who forced the three tyrants–Thanom, Prapas and Narong–to leave the country. After the 1932 abolition of the "absolute monarchy," the royal court had been largely ceremonial. However, in October, 1973 the army brought King Bhumibol, who enjoys national popularity similar to Queen Elizabeth, in to topple the old government.

The result was that no basic changes occurred in our political system. A civilian prime minister was appointed; he allowed freedom of the press. But the army controlled everything, including the police, who continued to check people's telephones, open their letters and watch their movements. One of the 1973 demands produced a new constitution within a year, but it was really no better than any previous version. The National Assembly which drafted it–elected from names nominated by the king–were mostly top bureaucrats and businessmen. Hardly anyone stood for the people, or understood their grievances.

During the first year of the new government, constant rumors of pending *coups d'etat* circulated; in fact, the government did resign once, but Prime Minister Sanya resumed his work again within a week with a few new faces in his cabinet. As the new government had no real power, the best it could do was to maintain the *status quo.*

Still the people, oppressed for so long, began to make demands through strikes and demonstrations and public debate as soon as the new sense of freedom arrived. The government, feeling itself only temporarily in power, could at best pacify the people. But it could not even reform the administration, much less tackle real problems like land reform for the benefit of the majority of Thai farmers.

Real grievances cannot be solved merely by establishing a constitution and parliament. These two institutions help to provide the basic framework for freedom and the rule of law, but as they are now they do not provide for real social justice.

The Thai, even in the time when the kings were sovereign, managed to live with freedom and dignity, as well as be *Sanuk* (remember? enjoying oneself). Does our future promise to return these possibilities to us?

Time alone will tell. Although the demands for justice have not been addressed meaningfully, and although democratic institutions are still alien to our soil, we do have now the rule of law, some kind of elected representatives and an opportunity to talk openly and carefully about the political system we want.

If the current government, or one of its type, can last for half a dozen years, we may be able to solve some fundamental problems in the short term.

In the long run perhaps we may be able to find a new political system which can be cultivated in our soil, suitable to our climate and beneficial to our people. Who knows?

BURMA: INTERCHANGE AND IDENTITY

U Kyaw Than

Pa-gan,* the eleventh century capital in central Burma, is well-known for its temple ruins exceeding 4 million Buddhist structures.[15] Within 16 square miles of the ancient city alone over 2,000 of the original 5,000 temples and pagodas provide a rare archeological paradise.

Once, visiting this historical resort for rest and reflection, General Ne Win asked an accompanying officer whether it was nobler to leave behind for posterity such monuments to morality, or to leave the means and conditions for a moral society.[16]

The General, himself a Buddhist, and caught in the national developments of mid-twentieth century Burma, was obviously meditating about the role a leader should play in molding the destiny of his peoples and enhancing peace and prosperity for the succeeding generations. In September, 1958 he had been called upon by then incumbent Premier U Nu to lead a caretaker government and to hold fair and free elections in the wake of the major split in the ruling political party. In April, 1960 the General handed the reins of government back to U Nu who was returned by an overwhelming popular vote in the elections duly conducted by the General's caretaker regime. By March, 1962 signs of struggle among the political factions and ethnic minorities led to a coup, and resumption of power by General Ne Win as head of a Revolutionary Council.

The immediate results were sharp regulation and limitation of

---

U Kyaw Than is known worldwide for his many years with the East Asia Christian Conference. After serving as Associate General Secretary from the EACC's beginning in 1959, he became general secretary in 1967 where he remained through 1973. In January, 1974 U Kyaw Than and his family left Bangkok to journey to Yale Divinity School where he will serve as Visiting Professor of Missions for three years. He has also worked with the World Student Christian Federation and the World Council of Churches as East Asia Secretary.

*Pa-gan (approximately A.D. 1044-1300), in the words of the March, 1971, *National Geographic*, "rhymes with anon and has nothing to do with our 'pagan,' as in pagan worship." (See footnote 15.)

international contact. Many outsiders responded to the "closed doors" by calling Burma a "hermit nation." A great curiosity has surrounded the questions: What are the hopes and ideals of Burma? What does it mean to be a Burman today? Has the process of closing off the outside helped to create the means for a moral society?

HISTORY'S OUTWARD AND INWARD THRUSTS

In the first place, world history provides many examples of isolationism in various forms. Modern-day China looked inward, as its ancestors did. Emperor Shih Huang Ti's development of the great wall of China in the third century B.C. is cited by some as a period of internal consolidation of China behind that great defense barrier. Others will argue that the closed-door policy of Japan's Tokugawa Shogunate led to the basic national integration of Japan's later advent in the international scene. Yet others may cite contemporary examples of "isolationism" between and within nations, initiated to achieve particular ideals and goals. The thought and life of any people cannot be analyzed only in terms of the immediate context. Some historical perspective, however brief, will be necessary in the effort to understand contemporary Burma.

A traveler flying into Rangoon, the present capital of Burma, will notice from the air, long before touching down at the airport, the glittering sight of Shwe-da-gon, the tall golden pagoda dating back to the sixth century B.C. Tradition holds that it enshrines four threads of hair handed over by the Buddha to two Burmese merchants who later returned from India with these relics.

Culturally Sanskrit and racially Mongolian, the Burman draws on the traditions of India on the one hand and the physical traits of the people of China on the other. The fusion of the influences from these two great neighbors is evident even in the daily dress of the Burmese males and females. The upper jacket is an adaptation of Chinese dress while the lower skirt is that of the Indian.

These components of the traditions, cultures and costumes of its neighbors have been adapted and developed into something peculiarly Burmese. The identity of the Burman has similarly emerged with distinctive characteristics as the ancient migrants moved down from the north and settled along the great river valleys of the area which became Burma, an area bounded by mountain ranges and plateaus on one side and the Indian ocean on the other. To be a Burman, therefore, involves being conscious of the great civilizations and racial origins of history but at the same time being aware of the identity and image which has emerged as a community and people through fusion, interchange and common struggle.

Yet it is not easy to express or define that self-consciousness or identity as a nation. The laws of the land and the values of monarchical dynasties, until the vanishment of the last king at the time of the British annexation of Burma in 1885, drew largely on the traditions of Burma's western neighbor, India. But the racial makeup of the people points toward China on Burma's northeastern flank. The eleventh century saw the emerging consolidation of Burma and that of the integration of the ethnic communities such as Mons, Shans and Karens into the growing nation. From the sixteenth to eighteenth centuries the nation expanded, reaching out and incorporating within its borders Arakan, Assam and Manipur (now part of India) in the west and north, and Siam and Laos in the east.

If that earlier period of Burmese history featured the *development* of the nation and national identity through absorption, interchange and fusion of external influences, cross-fertilization of cultures, and reaching out or expansion, the period between 1885 and 1948 or even the present characterized the *intensification* of national identity through crystallization and selection. The three Anglo-Burmese wars, culminating with the imposition of colonialism on Burma by the British in 1885, provided an unprecedented experience for the Burmese. It forced them to seek ways of throwing off the foreign yoke and reexpressing the national identity. The anti-British patriotic movement, with three-pronged emphasis on the preeminence of the nation, culture and religion underscored for the Burmans the danger they were in, unless the national heritage was redeemed from colonial captivity. As the British settled in, the Shans, a significant ethnic group in eastern Burma, were allowed by the British to continue to maintain their system of feudal chiefs and regional autonomy. The Burmese, the majority of the population, progressively secured certain reins of power and legislative initiatives. The outbreak of the Second World War and the excesses of the Japanese occupation of Burma provided new urgency to the common struggle by the Burmese and the ethnic minority groups to regain independence and selfhood.

This also demonstrated the need for establishing the "Union of Burma" as a federal republic and to give the term *Burman* an enlarged and more comprehensive connotation. After regaining independence the first President of the Union was a Shan: later a Karen was elected to hold that high office. When an extremist political faction assassinated the members of the State Executive Council, including General Aung San, the widely accepted national leader, distinguished members of different ethnic communities shared with him in the supreme sacrifice. To be a citizen of the Union of Burma is to recognize the identity which was the aggregate of the traditions, sentiments and aspirations of the various ethnic communities, whether Burman, Mon, Shan, Karen, Kachin or Chin. It also requires the readiness to transcend ethnic bias and to cultivate sensitivities to the import of Union citizenship. But Burma's development of such a new sense of nation needs time, understanding, favorable interaction among the groups and communities involved and solidarity of purpose. In

Burma's historical process, the earlier periods of "absorption and outreach" were followed by the latter period of "resistance" and "intensification of molding the national spirit." If the present state of regulated international intercourse means Burma's conscious adoption of the "hermit" role to take stock, reflect and consolidate, this may very well be a positive period in the history of the country.

FACTORS FOR AN IDENTITY MOLD

Some Religious Factors

Buddhism supplies a key ingredient to the national identity mold. Buddhism, particularly the Theravada or Hinayana school (as distinguished from the Mahayana of the Northern Buddhist countries) prevails in the country. Some Buddhist features are significant for understanding the orientation of the nation. Along with the Buddha and his teachings, the priesthood is revered as one of the Three Jewels. People look up to members of the priesthood for their renunciation of the world, continence, learning, asceticism, classless fellowship and collective sharing. Buddhist teaching emphasizes renunciation of the flesh and quenching of desire or attachment to the world's or history's things.

L. W. Pye, in his study of Burma entitled *Politics, Personality and Nation Building,* makes a telling statement about the British and American experience of Burma.

> India could confirm an Englishman in his values and convince him of the need and the justice of spreading his version of progress and development. Burma challenged his values by subtly bringing them into question and casting doubts as to whether effort and progress are really significant goals for human life. . . . India now suggests to Americans the urgency of five-year plans and the merits of modern industrial development, while Burma continues to evoke a question as to whether modern life is really the ultimate way. . . .[17]

The Constitution of 1947 recognized the special position of Buddhism in the Union of Burma as the faith professed by the great majority of Union citizens, while it also recognized Islam, Christianity, Hinduism and Animism as some of the religions existing in the Union at the date of the coming into force of the Constitution.[18] Later, U Nu, premier and a devout and ardent Buddhist, took special initiatives to hold the Sixth Buddhist Council at Rangoon during 1954-56 (the First Council had been held in approximately 544 B.C.). In 1961 he fulfilled his election pledge to amend the Constitution, making Buddhism the state religion. The Constitution ratified in 1973 under General Ne Win made no mention of a state religion. Instead, equality of all citizens before the law regardless of their religious affiliation and right to freedom of thought, faith and worship were reaffirmed more positively.[19] The reinstatement of Buddhist values had been a popular invocation during the nationalist struggle against colonial rulers. Some had come to claim that one had to be a Buddhist to be a Burman.

The 1973 Constitution emphasized that Burma would be a secular state with a socialist orientation. In struggling to be a nation true to its heritage while facing the challenges of history, Burma's socialist orientation had been defined in the particular national context.[20]

The Response of The Church

Traditionally Buddhism undergirds Burmese culture and nationalism. As mentioned earlier the patriotic movement had its three-pronged emphasis on the preeminence of the nation, culture and religion. Religion meant Buddhism. (It later led to the role Burma played in holding the Sixth Buddhist Council at Rangoon and the constitutional revision of 1961 to declare Buddhism as the State religion of Burma.) Because of the historical coincidence of the arrival of Protestant missionaries with that of the British colonial expansion into Burma, confusion remained in the attitude of Buddhists in Burma toward Christianity. Christianity, as the religion which started to have its impact on the people around the time of the British annexation of Burma, could not be seen by the majority, even decades afterwards, as an element which could be associated with national traditions or aspirations. For Burmans to accept Christ, leaving behind their Buddhist or animist backgrounds, the religious step taken involved giving up long-held beliefs and often the circle of close friends and relatives.

As the years passed and the number of indigenous Christians grew, and as they engaged more and more in the different services to the nation, attitudes began to change. As the church grew in spirit, strength and knowledge there was more openness and confidence in tackling practical as well as theological issues in the relation between Christian faith and culture and between church and society. The Japanese occupation provided an unprecedented opportunity to all nationals, Christian or Buddhist, to be thrown together in a common struggle against the aggressor. This led to the modification or breaking of the image of the association of the church with colonialism and enabled many to appreciate that Christian faith can provide the basis for patriotism in Burma and for participation by Christians in nation building.

But that opportunity for the development of a sense of solidarity among all nationals was marred later when some sectors of minority ethnic groups channeled their aspirations into separatist movements. Some demanded regional autonomy for themselves or complete secession from the Union of Burma in order not to be dominated by the majority sector of the population. Substantial numbers among one or two such groups happened to be Christian and this revived some of the old misunderstandings about the credibility of nationals who are not Buddhist.

Happily there were also articulate and active Christians who continued to share with the majority population in their national aspirations and to serve the nation as it moved forward to development goals after independence.

When the renewal of residence permits of foreigners was curtailed for those considered not deserving priority attention for favorable decisions by the authorities, the foreign missionary community was also affected. This became an issue for discussion among the Christians and attitudes toward this development differ according to the sentiments and political sophistication of the persons concerned. Words exchanged at the last farewell party held at Rangoon for the departing Baptist missionaries were indicative of the sentiments and attitudes of the leading Christians at that time. A former chief executive officer of the ancient capital of Mandalay and a key Baptist elder expressed the appreciation the national church had for the long period of fellowship and service the generations of foreign missionaries had provided in Burma, while a Burma-born missionary responded by pointing out that the departure of a handful of missionaries would not "rock the boat of the church" when one considered the thousand-fold larger number of full-time national church workers who would continue to serve church and society.

Note might also be taken of a few, not so well-known, factors concerning the church in contemporary Burma. As the program for giving recognition to the place of Buddhism in the nation gained momentum, proportionate subsidies to the Christian and other non-Buddhist communities were offered to ensure that every religious body received similar and fair attention from the national budget. All religious leaders (Buddhist or otherwise) having reached a certain seniority of responsibility were entitled to travel free on all national transport systems. During the time of annual church assemblies (the Baptists, for example, bring together thousands annually) special trains and reduced fares were provided by the state to facilitate matters for the delegates and participants throughout the whole country.

Some Economic Factors

The colonial period had brought about the modernization of administration, economy and communications. But the economy had been dominated by outsiders. Some benefits accrued to a few nationals. But sensitive patriots compared themselves to the unfortunate frogs who watched helplessly at the boggy base of the lotus plants while the winged butterflies swept in from afar to suck the nectar from the blossoms. The lion's share of the economy was in the hands of the firms with colonial connections. Indian and Chinese migrants filled the role of middlemen in a widespread chain of commerce. In 1962 the Revolutionary Council refused to renew the residence permits of foreigners with the exception of a few considered essential to development projects and plans. Many Chinese and Indian citizens left the country at that time.

In the agrarian sector of the national economy, a succession of Burmese administrators gave special attention to seeking solutions. Agricultural subsidies, tenancy conditions, regulations for absentee landlordism, land alienation and diversification of crops were all tried in the search for solving the agrarian problem. Different measures used in solving the agrarian problem led ultimately to the more drastic Land Nationalization Act. And progressive measures to protect the nationals from the more commercially astute and experienced foreign businessmen and firms culminated with the denial to them of residence and usual privileges for economic involvement within the country. And as the national firms and indigenous businessmen were not in command of adequate resources and initiatives, the method of more direct intervention and control by the state became the order of the day. Replacement of multiple and popular international intercourse by the more monolithic efforts of the state contributed again to the aspects of isolationism of the nation.

National development schemes have long existed for Burma, and the Pyi-daw-tha (Happy Land) convention of 1952 made formal the faith that eventually Burma's human and natural resources would lead the nation to balanced development.

One factor has intensified the pressure: Burma's high birth and declining death rates have accounted for a population growth from an estimated seventeen million in 1941 to an expected thirty-six million by 1980. Compared with its neighbors, Burma may not appear to have a problem; some would even argue that numbers of people are important for development. If the traditional rice surplus, and its market price (as well as other natural resources like teak and minerals) remain favorable for Burma, the asceticism of the hermit nation may not prove severe or pointless for its people.

THE EXPERIMENT CONTINUES

Yet the road ahead is still steep and the journey difficult. General Aung San, the martyred national leader who led Burma on the road to freedom and unity, reminded the nation in his last address (1947) that Burma, to maintain parity of development with other neighbors, must take four or five strides when others take just one step. "Even with constant application and backbreaking endeavor, it may take two whole decades before Burma can catch up with a moderately developing neighbor," he forewarned.[21]

U Ne Win (who exchanged his military title in 1973 for the Burmese "U," a title stronger than the English "mister"), the military and now the political heir of Bogyoke Aung San, seeks ways to leave a heritage which can provide the conditions for the emergence of a moral society whose members can enjoy peace and prosperity. His administration, in the eyes of observers, emphasizes asceticism in international intercourse, restraint in personal consumption and state initiative in the major fields of the national economy. Those who disagree with his approach argue that in the contemporary world the concerns for *identity* need to be held together with more spontaneous *interchange* with other identities. A nation may give priority to focusing on crystalizing its own identity in seclusion rather than through interchange, on withdrawal than on involvement, community welfare rather than individual freedom and corporate planning instead of personal initiative.

Others may regard these points of focus not so much as mutually exclusive variables, but as factors for an identity mold requiring different patterns of juxtaposition. How these factors are held together or how their interaction is regulated influence for good or ill the texture of a people's history and the national process. Burma's leadership at present has chosen a particularly Burmese pattern of socialist theory. They tried to consider Burma's history, its cultural heritage, the ethnic sentiments and relations, the present challenges of the economy and the pressures of national and world developments.[22]

Some may wonder whether the fourteen-year experiment still deserves the benefit of a doubt. Others point to the lack of an articulate and constitutionally acknowledged opposition. Yet others may point out that a carbon copy of democracies of the West is not something which will provide for the delivery of goods as Asian nations seek solutions to national problems. And there will also be those who will remind commentators that the 1973 Constitution has not yet had a chance to prove itself, and that a decade and two years (1962-1974) cover too short a period in the process of Burmese history to expect noticeable progress in the life of a nation which had encountered so many historical upheavals. Such include annexations or occupation, alien economic exploitation, shocking assassination of key leaders, multiple insurgency, dispatch of the general populace into "mothball" hybernation, and last.but not least, the intellectual struggle to reinstate an ancient philosophical system or to synchronize it with modern political theories.

The experiment is on. And only time will tell whether Burma creatively stood up to the challenges of history and utilized its human, philosophical and material resources for the benefit of posterity and for playing its contributive role in the family of nations.

MALAYSIA: RACE RELATIONS AND ECONOMICS

Lim Mah Hui

For over a thousand years the luxuriant tropical forests in Malaysia and the abundant life in its rivers and seas have supported a rich and varied population. A constant flux of people visited the Malay peninsula. Some left their marks and passed on. Others chose to settle. Through the centuries, fishermen and peasants from the Indonesian islands, farmers from China, Arab and Portuguese traders, villagers from Thailand came and enriched the culture.

The casual visitor to Malaysia is delighted to discover Malay kite-flying contests, Chinese lion dances and the Indian Thaipusam (Hindu religious event). The towns, with their collection of mosques, Buddhist and Hindu temples and Christian churches, all reinforce the picture of a truly multiracial society. Today Malaysia's population numbers over 12 million: 42 percent are Malays, 37 percent Chinese, 10 percent Indians, 8 percent Dyaks and other aboriginal groups and 3 percent others. Most of the Chinese and Indians have arrived only in the last 100 years.

The eleven states of West Malaysia and the two of East Malaysia are separated by 800 miles of ocean. Communication between them is poor; lingual, cultural and economic differences are considerable. West Malaysia itself has two distinct regions: the West Coast, covered with rubber and oil palm plantations, the remains of open-pit tin mines and fair-sized towns inhabited largely by Chinese and the East Coast, blanketed by jungle and dotted with Malay *kampongs* and fishing villages.

Malaysia has often been hailed as the melting pot of Asia. Beneath, however, the postcard image of a beautiful Malaysia with its peoples living

---

Lim Mah Hui teaches sociology at the University of Malaya and is the chairperson of the World Student Christian Federation for the Asian region in 1974-1975. After receiving an economics degree at the University of Malaya, Lim worked for the Student Christian Movement of Malaysia before going to the University of Pittsburgh where he completed an M.A. in Sociology and a Master's in Public and International Affairs. He is currently completing his doctoral work.

in harmony is the undercurrent of racial hostility which occasionally bursts out into the open. Malaysia's economics and politics are heavily affected by racial considerations.

Malaysia's political system is a mixture of the Malay feudal sultanate and the British Parliamentary institutions. Most of the political parties in Malaysia thrive on racial appeals.* Only one, the Pan Malaysian Islamic Party (PMIP), is solely communalistic. It seeks the creation of a Malay state based on Islamic law. The Alliance Party, in power since 1957 independence, is intercommunal, but at election time its separate divisions (United Malay National Organization, Malayan Chinese Association and Malayan Indian Congress) play on the communal fears of their respective communities.

Appeals to communities and races have inherent dangers. In Malaysia the tensions created by communal politics erupted into serious racial riots in May, 1969. The Chinese and Indians managed to win a considerable number of seats in the Parliament and seriously challenged the political power of the UMNO and the Malays. In fact, the predominantly non-Malay opposition parties were about to take over the three most important states of Malaysia. In this racially charged atmosphere, the overemotional and abusive behavior of a small group sparked off racial riots in the capital, Kuala Lumpur, which soon spread to other cities. By the end of the week over a thousand people were dead.**

The May, 1969 riots occurred because of the perceived threats that the Malays posed to the non-Malays and vice versa. While the non-Malays feared the political power of the Malays, the Malays resented the economic wealth of the Chinese. The British first created the dangerous myth that Malays control Malaysian politics while Chinese possess economic power. Foreign and national elites, who have taken over from the British the reigns of both political and economic control, have prolonged the myth.

Chinese businessmen are highly visible to Malay villagers. Many of the provision shops in the Malay *kampongs* are owned and run by Chinese. The middle people who buy the latex from the Malay rubber tappers are Chinese. The Malay who moves into town and finds a job in the factory is likely to have a Chinese foreman. Thus, although the Chinese own only 25

*This refers only to political parties in West Malaysia. For a fuller analysis of the relationship between political parties and communalism see K. J. Ratnam, *Communalism and the Political Process in Malaysia* (Kuala Lumpur: University of Malaya Press, 1965).

**It is unlikely that the details of what actually happened in the riots will ever be known. The government has refused to set up an independent commission to study the matter. For two different accounts see Tengku Abdul Rahman, *The May Thirteen Tragedy* (Kuala Lumpur: University of Malaya Press, 1970) and John Slimming, *Malaysia: Death of a Democracy* (London: John Murray, 1969).

percent of the economic wealth in Malaysia, the ordinary Malay thinks it is the Chinese who are exploiting. Malay political leaders and foreign businessmen are all too happy to encourage this belief.

FOREIGN ECONOMIC CONTROL

A close study of the facts shows how badly distorted the economic situation has been. Foreigners, together with a small national elite, own and control the economy of Malaysia. Seventy percent of the large plantations are owned by foreigners. The corporations in the industrial sector are nearly 60 percent foreign owned and controlled. Furthermore, much of Malaysia's wealth is siphoned off overseas at a tremendous rate–approximately $200 to $400 million every year. For example, between 1955 and 1961 the outflow of funds from Malaysia amounted to $1.54 billion or 10 percent of the Gross Domestic Produce for the same period.[23] Thus, although Malaysia has political independence, economically it is still a colony.

The small group of local economic elites, mainly Chinese, own about 25 percent of the remaining economic wealth. They represent only about 3 percent of the Chinese population. Income in Malaysia is very unevenly distributed. Only a tiny portion of the population is well-off. Sixty percent of the total households in Malaysia live on less than $80 a month, while only 1.4 percent earn more than $600 a month. (The average size of the Malaysian household is six.) The distribution of income within each race is even more skewed. About 0.4 percent of the Malay population earn more than $600 a month, and about 2.5 percent of the Chinese earn the same amount.[24]

ORIGINS OF THE RACE CONFLICT

The racial conflict in Malaysia is quite different from that in the United States. One race has not discriminated against another on the basis of color; neither has one enslaved the other. Furthermore, one race has not oppressed the other by a preponderance of economic and political power.

The race conflict in Malaysia arises primarily out of the identification of each race with certain economic categories, such as occupations or income. Most of the businessmen, professionals and middle-class people are Chinese and Indians living in the urban areas. Most of the Malays are peasants and fishermen living in the rural areas. Beyond these generalizations, there are, of course, many Chinese and Indians who form a major part of the industrial and agricultural plantation working class, with Malays making up a major portion of the civil service. This coincidence of economic and racial imbalance which developed under the British colonial rule is the major cause of Malaysian racial conflict.

Before the nineteenth century, Malaya was a homogenously and sparsely populated country, occupied mainly by Malays and aboriginal groups. Under British rule the subsistent agricultural economy ot Malaya was transformed into a rich rubber and tin producing economy. To do this the British encouraged unrestricted immigration and mass importation of cheap labor. Chinese and Indians came by the tens of thousands to build railroads, to operate the tin mines and to tap the rubber trees. They brought with them their languages, cultures, customs, educational systems, architectural styles, dresses and religions. There was little attempt at assimilation, especially since the rigid adherence to Islam by the local Malays discouraged intermarriage. There was minimal contact between the races except on official business. Even diet separated them–the Chinese relishing pork in many of their dishes, the Malays despising the filthy food forbidden in the Koran.

The British encouraged such compartmentalization in many ways and for obvious reasons. The creation of racial sentiments would tend to discourage the emergence of any form of class consciousness or anti-colonial feelings. The British not only encouraged segregation but also played one race against the other.

They granted the Malays special political privileges and concessions in order to allay their fears of the immigrants. The Malay Sultanate institution was preserved in form, although sultans lost all political power. The Malay College in Kuala Kangsar was established to prepare the children of the Malay aristocrats for positions in the Malay Civil Service, thus developing a small Malay administrative class. The majority of the Malay population was left untouched in the rural areas.

The Chinese businessmen became the functionaries who serviced the economy, while the Malay and Indian elites serviced the administrative machinery. Thus the upper and middle classes of the Malays, Chinese and Indians were content to receive a share of the wealth and power.

While the lower classes were exploited by siphoning off their surplus wealth, they were encouraged to develop a false consciousness. Malay peasants saw the Chinese as the source of their economic woes and as a threat to the Malay culture. The Chinese masses saw the Malays with special political privileges which imposed the Malay culture on them. Racial animosity gradually built up among the lower classes, while among the upper and middle classes, other common economic and social values mitigated the racial antagonism. Just as in Ireland, Nigeria, Cyprus, India and Palestine, the British left a country depleted of many of its natural resources and its people divided into two hostile camps.

MALAYSIA'S FUTURE

What does the future hold for Malaysia? The "May '69" riots jolted the Alliance government from its position of confidence and caused it to embark on a "New Economic Policy." It aims to restructure the economy, eliminating the identification of race with economic function. Among the

Children relax in the yard of a home in rural Malaysia.

targets set are the modernization of rural life, the establishment and expansion of the Malay commercial and industrial community, and the achievement of 30 percent ownership of industrial shares by Malays by 1990.[25]

Will the New Economic Policy solve the economic and racial problems of Malaysia? The logic of the policy is the creation of new Malay upper and middle classes to balance the present ones. Clearly such a policy does not solve the problem of poverty among the lower classes of all races. The people of these classes, whose resources are pitifully scarce, tend to see any gain by one section of a community as a loss to the other. Their competition for a better life is often translated into racial conflicts. During the "May '69" riots the lower class Chinese and Malays suffered the highest loss of life and property.

The result of the development efforts of the Alliance government has so far been to encourage the further concentration of wealth in the hands of the upper minority of the population. Since 1957 income distribution in Malaysia has become more unequal. Between 1957 and 1970 the share of the total Gross National Product of the top 10 percent of the population has increased from 34.1 percent to 39.7 percent, while that of the lower 20 percent has decreased from a meager 5.8 percent to 4.0

percent. In short, the rich have become richer and the poor, poorer. Even if the government succeeded in achieving the 30 percent Malay ownership of the economy, this 30 percent of the wealth will be owned by no more than 3 percent of the Malay population. The creation of a small upper and middle class among the Malays is no way to solve the problem of poverty among the Malay masses.

As long as the majority of the Malays, Chinese and Indians remain poor and are encouraged to view their economic plight in racial terms, racial conflicts will remain. The task ahead is to educate the people to understand that the source of racial conflict lies in economic inequality and social injustice. The economic and social injustice is created and maintained by an upper class that tends to benefit from it, irrespective of race. Malaysia's future hope lies in the conscientization and unification of the lower classes of all races against the upper classes who maintain this system of economic and racial exploitation.

VIETNAMESE WOMEN AND THE STRUGGLE FOR PEACE

Tue Hien Morrow

Many of you may wonder why President Nguyen Van Thieu has been in power for such a long time in South Vietnam. We Vietnamese wonder too. We often console ourselves half in fun by saying that the present sad

---

Tue Hien Morrow studied at the film workshop at Simon Fraser University in Vancouver, B.C. during the 1974-1975 school year. Born in Hanoi, she graduated from the "Free Pacific Institute" in Cholon, South Vietnam, then took a B.A. in Sociology at the National Taiwan University in Taipei. She married Michael Morrow who was covering the Vietnam war for *Dispatch News Service International* and worked as a Vietnamese and Chinese interpreter until her husband was expelled from Vietnam in 1970. For two years they traveled extensively in Southeast Asia and in 1973 Tue Hien began seriously to work in film. Tue Hien originally read this paper at a Quaker International Seminar in December, 1973, in Thailand.

situation of our country is due to the mistakes of our ancestors, who, indeed, had aggressively conquered and assimilated the Chams (tribe) and Cambodians. President Thieu is from Pham Ranh, the Chams' area. People say we have to suffer from the revenge of the Chams. This is a sad joke, but it is a joke, and it says something very important about Vietnamese men and women. Vietnamese have the ability to make the best of a bad situation. Most of our history, we have been under foreign domination or at war. Nonetheless, we still sincerely believe that history will bring victory to our people. And we keep on struggling. We call this struggle a struggle for peace.

To be truthful, most Vietnamese don't know what peace is. When we speak of peace, it's like talking about heaven, or at least a better world where the family is together, death is not so close, it is easier to make a living and, most of all, where we have some control over our own destiny. When we speak of peace, we really mean liberation. And when we speak of struggle, we sometimes mean war. Our history is bittersweet and our lives are filled with contradictions. It is particularly true for women because woman's role has been mixed up and made flexible by a history of war and oppression.

You may ask: What has this war done to our women and what have our women contributed toward peace? But before trying to answer these questions, we have to go back to the past to understand a little about Vietnamese woman's place in the history and culture of the country. What are the national characteristics of Vietnamese women, what roles do women play and what place do they have in our society? Traditionally, what has been their place in making Vietnamese history?

A well-known Vietnamese woman novelist once wrote: "Sometimes having wealth makes the mind poor. And being poor makes the mind rich. . . .It is also true that war makes life poor, but it enriches the soul's potential and the sentiment of women."

In reality, the long legacy of war and oppression has made the roles of women in national life more complicated and difficult. But it also made the roles more interesting and meaningful. War has created in women new capabilities to confront the obstacles of life.

RELATIONSHIP BETWEEN MEN AND WOMEN

To talk about the relationship between men and women in our society, first remember that Vietnam has been occupied many times by Chinese, Mongols, French and Americans. In terms of cultural contribution, the Chinese occupation of about 1,000 years is most important. During these 1,000 years Confucianism was exceptionally strong in China and many of its cultural concepts were transferred to Vietnam and became imbedded in Vietnamese culture. Among the most important is the strong distinction between male and female roles and between various social levels in society. However, it is also true that the Vietnamese keep very close to themselves a contradictory pattern of relationships. This pattern is very familiar and personal compared with the stiff and impersonal convention of Confucianism.

Thus, between male and female, there is a certain ambivalence. There are Confucianist ideas by which women are considered inferior in natural talents and social class. They are obliged to follow the dictates of a male world. On the other hand, there is a more Vietnamese idea, that the relationship between men and women is basically that of *Anh*, brother, and *Cei*, sister. In conversation, for example, it is common to drop the more formal titles of Chinese origin which correspond to Mister, Madam, Master or Sir–even when we do not know a person very well. When husband and wife present one another to a third person, Vietnamese just call one another *"Nha Toi,"* which means "my spouse," while Chinese use the terms *"Nei Nhan"* for wife and *"Oai Nhan"* for husband. *"Nei Nhan"* means a person who stays inside the house, *"Oai Nhan"* means the person who goes outside.

CONCEPT OF RESPONSIBILITY

The Vietnamese girl is taught always to be responsible. In the family, often a little girl about five or six years old is put in charge of her younger sisters or brothers. When the parents go out to work, the girl looks after her younger brothers and sisters and does some light housework. At the same time, the younger brothers and sisters are told to listen to the older sister–particularly young boys. As they grow up the attitude of accepting female advice or orders becomes natural. Vietnamese women often appear exceptionally "feminine" in the role of "sister." This is often soft or submissive on the outside, while inside, women more often than men have a sense of direction, and command enough respect if not fear from their men to mobilize a family, or some other social group, and accomplish their objectives. This may be where the concept "dragon lady" arises.

But "responsibility" does not mean freedom in the Western sense. Because of this deeply held notion of being responsible for the welfare of our families and husbands, we Vietnamese women have a very weak notion of our own ego or individual self. Individual interest is not separated from that of family and husband. That also means that when Vietnamese women involve themselves in national affairs, they take with them a similar idea and tend to involve themselves totally and with a feeling of loyalty to their particular cause, rather than concern for their own welfare.

Throughout history, women have been praised highly in our society for their virtues. Most of these relate to responsibility, being resourceful

A Vietnamese woman refugee carries her possessions along a road in the Delta away from the fighting in her village.

and hard working. The Vietnamese woman is supposed to be devoted to family, loyal to husband and children. Because of the loose role in the family, women in fact have more responsibilities than men.

WOMEN'S ROLE IN HISTORY

Among the first and most famous heroic leaders of Vietnam's struggle for independence were the Trung sisters. About 2,000 years ago, the Vietnamese were dominated by the Chinese Han Dynasty. Vietnam was severely ruled by Chinese; people were ruthlessly exploited. Many Vietnamese army officers were replaced by Vietnamese of Chinese origin because the Central Administration in China believed that the former were less loyal to China.

The Trung sisters were from a rich family–both had been trained in the martial arts. The older sister, Trung Trac, was married to Dang Thi Sach, a general stationed in Chai-Dien.

To Dinh, an officer of Chinese background, was elected Commander-in-Chief of Giao-Chi, a province near where Trung Trac and her husband lived. To Dinh was greedy and often exploited people in the province. The people had no way to oppose Dinh's will, and they took his hatred in silence. Dang Thi Sach, Trung Trac's husband, intervened many times on behalf of the people. He soon became the speaker for the people, and was respected as their leader against the evil Chinese General To Dinh. To Dinh finally killed Dang Thi Sach.

With deep grief for the people and a wish to revenge her husband's death, Trung Trac, with her sister Trung Nhi, called the people to arms to drive the Chinese out of Vietnam. They did throw To Dinh back to China and regained control of many provinces. The sisters established a new dynasty and led the country as the Trung Queens.

They did not stay in power long because of a strong counterattack from China and their own domestic problems. But the two sisters did in fact free the Vietnamese from repression for a short time. Their bravery brought lasting honor to Vietnamese women, and they set a precedent for future women leaders in many independence struggles.

As a Vietnamese historian has summarized in writing of a period from the end of the Trieu dynasty until the Ngo dynasty (about 1,000 years, until A.D. 938), male administrators yielded obediently without a single event of resistance against the Chinese oppressors. They were a shame to the country's history, particularly when compared with the Trung sisters who braved all to bring the nation freedom.

PRESENT ROLE IN THE STRUGGLE

There are many women figures in our present struggle, like Madame Nguyen Thi Binh, the Foreign Minister of the Provincial Revolutionary Government, a diplomat between war and peace; General Nguyen Thi Dinh, a commander of the National Liberation Front; Madam Ngo Ba Thanh, who has been put in jail many times for her strong struggle for peace and reconciliation; and Nhat Chi Mai, a young girl who burned herself in 1967 to protest the war. Thousands and thousands of women political prisoners have been tortured just because they want peace!

The Vietnamese epic poem, "Kim Van Kieu," written in the eighteenth century, is probably the most important piece of literature in understanding the contemporary Vietnamese mind. This famous narrative poem was written by Ngugyn Du, often called the revolutionary poet. "Kim Van Kieu" is known by virtually every Vietnamese, regardless of his or her status in life. It is considered the national poem.

In "Kim Van Kieu," human destiny is proclaimed: we have no hold on the future, but are born to suffer for the family. It tells of the beautiful Thuy Kieu who loved Kim Trong, but became a concubine of the ruthless merchant Ma Giam Sinh in return for money she needed to save her father from an unscrupulous tax collector. Accepting her fate, Kieu said: "It is better that I should sacrifice myself alone. It matters little if a flower fall if the tree can keep itself green."

In the poem, Thuy Kieu plays the roles of prostitute, student's mistress, servant, Buddhist nun, a victorious revolutionary's wife and other characters. She undergoes ravishment, sacrifice, glory and betrayal. Despite all of this, she manages to keep her soul intact. At one point she says, "The source of good lies in our hearts, and the heart, by itself, is worth three times more than talent."

To the young people of Vietnam, the meaning is clear: they must accept whatever hardships come so that the honor of the family and the country is preserved. Many Vietnamese girls who became prostitutes of American GI's saw themselves as modern-day Thuy Kieus, selling their bodies, but not their souls, to help their families.

In the poem, Kim Trong marries Thuy Kieu's sister, Thuy Van, but he never forgets his first love. Kim Trong finally finds Thuy Kieu after searching for many years. At the banquet celebrating Thuy Kieu's return, her sister proposes that Kim Trong and Thuy Kieu should now marry as they planned before fate intervened fifteen years before. In this scene Thuy Kieu is in a similar state, as is Vietnam today. Her body has been "battered by many storms," been fought over and sold to strangers, but through it all "filial piety" and love of family have persisted, and thus her soul has remained pure.

Vietnamese are fond of images of beauty and moral purity in the midst of corrupt and ugly surroundings. Beautiful vignettes from Ngugyn Du's story of Thuy Kieu are often recalled by Vietnamese to help them endure the corruption and the destruction which war has brought to their country, and to assure them that it is still possible to lead pure and beautiful lives, even in the midst of all the ugliness that war brings.

Life is seen by Vietnamese women as bittersweet and filled with contradiction. But the Vietnamese woman has faith in herself, or, at least, in her ability to endure and struggle. This is essential in understanding Vietnamese women today. This is a sentimental notion, which sometimes gives way to self-pity or becomes a rationalization. But it is perhaps the key to the resilience that is so basic to her character.

SOUTHEAST ASIA – THE ECONOMIC DIMENSION

Lee Soo Ann

From early times, Southeast Asia's economic activity has been determined largely by the need to be self-sufficient in the densely populated settlements separated from each other by sea or highlands. The region is crisscrossed by river valleys cutting through highlands or mountain ranges, but from the air there is a refreshing uniformity in the blanket of green which appears to be everywhere. The tropical climate provides thick forested inland areas and mangrove swamps nearer the coast, making sea access generally difficult except through river basins. In the fertile river valleys, rice was the staple cereal, supplemented by fish, vegetables, fruits, timber, coconuts and other ubiquitous plants. On such agrarian foundations grew the great historical empires, such as Srivijaya, Majapahit and Khmer.

The present-day economies of Southeast Asia, while still containing pockets of the traditional early agriculture and fishing, reflect more the results of expansionist colonial activity in the last three or four centuries. Although the countries in the region were colonized by different powers, essentially the purpose was the same–to obtain raw materials and markets for the emerging industries of the West. Existing crops were expanded to produce commercially, such as sugar in Indonesia, or to introduce new commodities, like rubber in Malaysia. New methods replaced old ones: tin-mining dredges owned by British companies worked side by side with the conventional gravel-pump mining in West Malaysia. Some parts of

---

Lee Soo Ann is associate professor of economics, University of Singapore. Among many church and community involvements, Dr. Lee is chairman of the Presbyterian urban and industrial mission work in Singapore. Author of *Industrialization in Singapore* and *Economic Growth and the Public Sector in Malaya and Singapore: 1948-60* and many articles, he did his undergraduate and doctoral work at the University of Singapore while taking a master's degree from Williams College in the U.S.

Southeast Asia, particularly Burma and Thailand, were less exploited, but by the start of World War II most of the region was under political control of the Western powers: Britain, France, America, Holland and Germany.

During World War II, Japanese occupation of much of the region not only laid the seeds of political change thereafter (by demonstrating that an Asian country could win militarily), but also opened the possibility of Southeast Asian countries developing economic ties among themselves and with Japan. The Japanese, during their brief occupation of the area (1942-45), attempted to organize Southeast Asia into a co-prosperity economic region.

When the countries became independent after World War II, development plans were instituted and manufacturing industries started to substitute local goods for imports. In Indonesia many foreign concerns were nationalized in an attempt to build up indigenous management and professional expertise. University education, neglected during colonial rule, was expanded for national use.

The new nations faced such basic problems as mounting population pressure, fluctuating markets for existing agricultural and mineral products and vast expanses of forested or otherwise unexploited land.

Large scale immigration, especially from India and China encouraged by the colonial rulers of labor-short Southeast Asian countries to sustain the required commercial output, ended after the war. The immigrants settled down in the countries to which they had come and shared responsibility with their indigenous neighbors for the high rate of population growth: 2.4 percent during the 1950's, 2.6 percent in the 1960's and a projected 2.9 percent for the 1970's.*

The region's existing agricultural and mineral products–tin, timber, rubber, oil palm, coconut oil, kenaf, etc.,–are largely intermediate in the world production process, having a "low value proportion" to the final product. Demand prospects in the long term are not predictably secure.

In the decades of the fifties and sixties the resurgent economies, especially of Japan and Western Europe together with the continuing strength of the American economy, sustained the level of commodity prices and encouraged even greater Southeast Asian production of these commodities. In Malaysia this took the form of extensive rubber replanting and new planting, as well as the introduction of oil palm on a commercial basis.

Although the world picture for commodities is not unduly pessimistic, the basic problem still remains: although supply is steady, there are short-term shifts in demand due to stockpiling and business booms. Commodity prices can fluctuate considerably from month to month or

*See Appendix C, "Population and Per Capita Income in Southeast Asian Countries" for references to population and per capita income.

year to year. Given the dominance of commodity production in the economies of many Southeast Asian nations, with much of government revenue based on commodity-based taxation, it is difficult to plan for the long term.

Because of its strategic location, Singapore has always been the major port of the region, and in the last decade it has increased its economic strength through a well-formulated program of industrialization and improvement of its communications and transport facilities. Many foreign firms and multinational corporations have either established regional headquarters or located manufacturing plants there. Singapore is the only port which can receive container vessels and repair large ships in Southeast Asia. Recently it has opened its doors to foreign banks and is now the leading Asian dollar market center.

East and West Malaysia are separated by the South China Sea: the former has only a small population but large timber resources while the latter has successfully specialized in rubber, supplemented by rice, oil palm, coconut and tin production. (West Malaysia was formerly Malaya; in 1963 Sarawak and Sabah were added to form Malaysia.) It has also started a successful industrialization program and has achieved self-sufficiency in oil and rice.

Indonesia is too large a country to be adequately described in a few paragraphs. Its major islands–Kalimantan, Celebes, Sumatra and Java–are largely self-contained economies. Stretching over two thousand miles from east to west and about a thousand miles from north to south, this potentially rich economy is held together thinly by coastal shipping and a fledgling national airline.

After the fall of President Sukarno in 1965 Indonesia opened its doors to Western and Japanese markets, to technology and capital. Its vast mineral resources are now beginning to be exploited on a large scale as continual new discoveries and prospecting revise expectations. The recently discovered Kasim oil field in Irian Jaya (Indonesian New Guinea), for example, is believed to have the biggest reserves outside the Middle East.

The most fertile island is Java where half of Indonesia's population cultivates rice, cassava (a tapioca plant), coffee, coconut, tobacco, sugar and spices. The other islands are rich in mineral resources, and some foothill zones have been developed for rubber and other commercial crop production. Indonesia faces such problems as how to find ways to keep the prices of their commodities more stable and how to integrate its economy; for example, moving labor and capital from overpopulated to newly developed areas and using the resources of the outer islands to benefit the population.

There is a shortage of middle and high-level management and

technically proficient personnel. In the past, higher education has not been geared to the needs of a capitalistic-oriented development strategy.

With the majority of the population untouched by the pockets of development, inequities in income distribution develop on top of the inevitable exploitation of the numerous weak by the strong few.

The Philippine archipelago, too, has the problem of developing on an agricultural base, but lacks the oil and mineral wealth of Indonesia. Their main exports—copra, sugar and timber—are barely sufficient to pay for their industrial requirement imports. Shortly after World War II the Philippines embarked on an ambitious import-substitution industrialization program. The industrialization programs of Malaysia and Singapore, in comparison, are slightly different. Although initiated to replace imports of consumer goods, they developed into production for export markets, thereby obviating foreign exchange difficulties.

Like the Philippines, Thailand exports part of its agricultural produce, principally rice. Tourism and American military expenditures arising out of the Vietnam war have given additional income. The economic future of Thailand, more so than Malaysia, Singapore, Indonesia and the Philippines, will be affected by the activities along its sensitive borders with China, Laos and Cambodia.

The Southeast Asian economic future will depend not only on what each country does, in terms of mobilization of productive resources, discipline, political stability and farsighted leadership, but also on external economic relationships. The landlocked nature of Laos and the closed-door policy of Burma make these countries less susceptible to external factors. The war in South Vietnam and Cambodia make it difficult to predict their future.

The external economic relationships of Southeast Asian countries are principally with Japan and the United States. These economic giants have found it profitable to invest and trade with Southeast Asia because of the availability of consumer markets and the opportunities for mineral and agricultural resource development. By 1971, some 23 percent of accumulated Japanese overseas direct investment had gone to Southeast Asia, compared to 16 percent each to Western Europe and Latin America. The proportion is somewhat lower for American overseas direct investment, being only 6 percent. But Southeast Asia had a trade surplus with the United States of $846 million in 1972, in contrast to a $830 million trade deficit with Japan.

Japanese goods—Hondas, Sonys, Datsuns and thousands of other names—abound in Southeast Asian cities and developed areas. Both Japanese and American industrial investment can be found in Southeast Asian countries with import-substitution industrialization programs, since direct investment can benefit from tax and other incentives. Japanese investment has, in addition, gone into resource development and extraction because of its heavy dependence on overseas supplies of raw materials and fuel. The value of Southeast Asian exports to Japan are therefore likely to overtake those to the United States soon.

United States economic influence, nevertheless, will continue to remain strong because of American economic strength on the world scene and the activities of American-based multinational corporations.

Both Japan and the United States receive a significant share of the exports of Southeast Asia and, to a lesser extent, the imports into the region. The center of economic interest has therefore shifted to the Pacific basin from Western Europe. To counter present Japanese and American economic influence, some Southeast Asian countries are actively cultivating European interest in investment. Singapore and Indonesia, for example, are looking to Britain and Holland, their old colonial exploiters, for more investments.

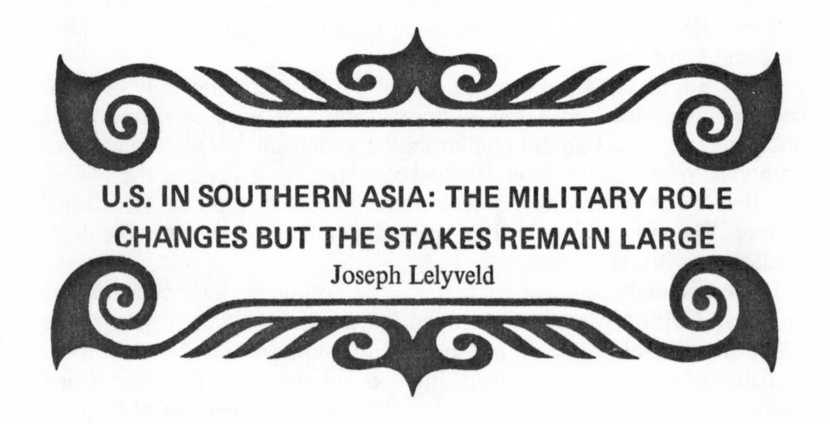

U.S. IN SOUTHERN ASIA: THE MILITARY ROLE CHANGES BUT THE STAKES REMAIN LARGE

Joseph Lelyveld

The United States is gradually reducing its commitments in Asia but rapidly expanding its interests as it gropes, almost in a somnambulant manner, for a new role in the region.

In the aftermath of the combat operations in Indochina, themes that

---

Joseph Lelyveld is based in Hong Kong for *The New York Times*. From there he travels widely in Southeast Asia as well as observing China from the Hong Kong porthole. His assignments with the *Times* have included covering South Africa, Zairé, New Delhi, Pakistan and Sri Lanka. To write a series of articles, from which this book takes one excerpt, he visited ten countries over a five-month period. This article is reprinted from the June 23, 1974 edition of *The New York Times*, by special permission of *The New York Times*.

justified the American stance in Asia for two decades–militant anti-communism and self-proclaimed altruism–appear to have been played out.

One by one assumptions on which American diplomacy built an elaborate security system in the nineteen-fifties were discarded: First in the Nixon doctrine in 1969, with its assumption that the United States would avoid a direct combat role in Asian conflicts; then in the dramatic American end run to Peking two years later, which stunned Japan and all the other Asian nations that had been evangelized by the United States and offered protection against the menace from China.

Now even the fallback position of the Nixon doctrine is eroding, for every Congressional assault on a military aid bill imposes new limitations and conditions on the promise that the United States would continue to funnel indirect military support to its old Asian allies. Asians find that American officials no longer hazard assurances on long-range American intentions.

But if American intentions are obscure now, American power is not. On the contrary, the solidity of the American presence–as seen in ten Asian nations over a period of five months–makes a striking contrast to the tentativeness of American attitudes. . . .

The real momentum for an expansion of American interests showed up in investment and business. For just when Asia, and Southeast Asia in particular, was becoming synonymous with disaster in the imagination of most Americans, American based multinational corporations were discovering an alluring frontier for expansion and profit.

"It's not a withdrawal, it's an invasion," a bemused Malaysian official declared.

If there is disengagement, it is mainly in a sense of detachment from the worsening social tensions and mass poverty that afflict many Asian countries: American development assistance to the region is less than half of what it was in 1964, on the eve of the major commitment of American forces to Vietnam.

MILITARY: NEARING NORMAL

However, the widely predicted military disengagement is still only a prediction. Indeed, if 1964, the year of the Tonkin Gulf incident, is taken as a reference point, the American military posture can be described as returning to normal.

Despite the withdrawal of 650,000 troops from Asia over five years, American military strength in Southeast Asia is still marginally greater than it was then. . . .

[There] is a strategic premise that has survived for a generation–that the United States needs conventional forces in Asia to have non-nuclear "options" in future, as yet unimagined, crises.

The long-term American role in the region, as explained in the Nixon doctrine, is to counterbalance threats posed by other nuclear powers, the Soviet Union and China. But strategic theorizings still take second place to the continuing preoccupation with Indochina. The comparison with the 1964 force levels shows a marked shift in the center of gravity in the American presence toward Southeast Asia.

In 1964 the American economic stake in Asia, outside Japan, could reasonably have been called negligible. No one would say that now. In ten years American trade with the region has doubled while equity investments have increased threefold.

At a conservative estimate American corporations have put $3.5-billion into Asia excluding Japan; the value of their assets–the figures are unavailable–is significantly higher.

The surge was led by electronics concerns that discovered ten years ago that they could undercut their Japanese competitors by hiring young Asian women to assemble components flown from the United States and then flown right back. They have been followed in the last five years by the big leaguers–the oil companies, the auto makers and a legion of banks rushing into their first Asian ventures.

BIG INVESTMENTS FOR OIL

Leading the international scramble, the American oil companies will spend several hundred million dollars this year on exploration in the Java Sea and the Gulf of Siam. The "exposure" of American banks in the region–that is, the amount they have out on loan–is more than $6-billion outside Japan, banking sources estimate, and is steadily rising.

At last count five hundred American companies, big and small, had opened offices in Hong Kong. Singapore, which has developed a short-term, high-interest Asian dollar market, has sixteen American banks with branches or representative offices scouting for business. There are eighty-eight companies there connected with the oil industry-drilling contractors, equipment suppliers, rig builders and those engaged in exploration.

That the United States is coming out of its Vietnam trauma with a vastly larger stake in the area than it had when it went to war is just the first of a series of paradoxes that show up in the new pattern of relations. The most painful is the most enduring–Vietnam itself.

The American troops have left, taking their massive firepower with them, and 135,000 Vietnamese have been laid off by American agencies of all kinds. Yet Americans arriving in South Vietnam are startled to hear old Saigon hands assert that, fundamentally, nothing has changed in the relations between Saigon and Washington–that the dependence remains total, with no end in sight. . . .

Vietnamese, asked to leaf back through earlier chapters of the endless struggle to find a point of comparison for the American role in 1974, almost invariably hit upon the year 1962 or 1963, the last years of President Ngo Dinh Diem, when a heavy commitment of American combat troops was still held to be an unthinkable prospect.

The implications of this comparison are unthinkable in the American perspective but self-evident to the Vietnamese–that in the event of a sudden deterioration of the military situation, Washington could be faced, yet again, with a decision whether to intervene. . . .*

NO CHANGE IN ATTITUDE

"The Americans still want a government that is openly and officially pro-American," said a Vietnamese, a dissident professor named Ton That Thien who served Mr. Diem as press secretary. . . .

"The basic attitude of the Americans hasn't changed," he said when asked to compare 1962-63 and 1974. "Basically nothing has changed–except that now, thanks to the Americans, we have on our hands one million Hondas with no gasoline to put in them, a huge state apparatus with no money to pay for it and a bigger war, in which Vietnamese do all the dying.". . .

The paradox of the American presence in Asia–of power wrapped in ambiguous intentions–is nowhere more evident than in Thailand, where, at last count, the United States had thirty-five military commands. In terms of current operations, the Air Force units in Thailand are restricted to reconnaissance flights over Indochina and support drops for the forces of the Lon Nol Government in Cambodia–daily transfusions that enable it to maintain its tenuous hold on life. In the last year, American military aid to Cambodia has amounted to at least $570-million. . . .

In the past it was assumed that Thai public opinion was adequately reflected in the attitudes of the generals with whom the Americans reached the series of unwritten understandings on which the complex military presence was built. What was unpredictable, officials would say, was American opinion.

But a student upheaval here last October [1973] produced a new Constitution and the promise of an election in which the bases will inevitably figure as an issue. In this context it was Thai opinion, as manifested in student groups that have periodically become inflamed over the American presence, that produced the reduction of it.

Oddly enough, while Thai public opinion was taken for granted, there was never much of an effort to shape a rationalization for the bases from a

*Lelyveld's insight in June, 1974 was proved out in January, 1975–as this book goes to press–as a deteriorating military situation in South Vietnam and Cambodia led to renewed reconnaisance and supply flights by American military and private-contract planes into Cambodia and Vietnam, as well as conversations in Washington about additional aid to the two countries.

Thai point of view. On the contrary, American officials took pains to assure Congress that the Thais understood that the American forces were here not for the defense of Thailand but simply because, as the last American Ambassador, Leonard Unger, testified in 1969, Vietnam had become "overcrowded."

Now it is being asked why Thailand should be so acquiescent and available to the Americans.

"The United States has confessed its inability to continue with its old policies," said Thanat Khoman, a former Foreign Minister who was for years the most articulate defender of the American presence. "Who are we, a small country like Thailand, to continue to adopt a cold war posture? The United States has the discretion to change. Why cannot we?". . .

The proof of the pervasiveness of the American influence can be found in the opposition to the bases: The fact is that a critical awareness of the American military presence was imported, like the planes themselves, from the United States.

The first account of the bases published in the Thai language was a reprint of a 1966 speech by Senator J. W. Fulbright that appeared in an influential journal, *The Social Sciences Review*, which has continued to use material supplied by American peace groups in its effort to build resistance to the bases among students and intellectuals.

It is not just the data that come from the United States. To a surprising degree the political consciousness that gave rise to the student movement last fall had its origins in the experiences of Thais who were studying on American campuses when the peace movement was at its zenith.

"Our social consciousness came through English," said Sumalee Viravaidya, the only woman to serve on the committee that drafted the Constitution. In her own case it came in Bloomington, Ind., when, as a student at Indiana University, she watched with a bewildered sense of injury as her American friends became involved in the antiwar movement.

"I thought the Americans were defending my country," she said. "They were saying it was wrong for the Americans to defend my country."

By the time she came home in 1968, she was opposed to the war and opposed to the American use of Thai bases.

Young Thais who have followed the same route often say they see the bases now as a symptom of a deeper malady–Thailand's lopsided distribution of political and economic power. That leads them to ask whether the removal of the symptom might not deepen the malady by provoking another military take-over. As much as anything else, that doubt buys time for the American force.

Sometimes it almost seems that the United States has become the main source of the subversive influence against which it has been seeking all those years to immunize Asia. American academic critiques of development theories or American controversies over multinational corporations can have a more direct impact on Asian political debates than revolutionary rhetoric from Peking.

Indonesian students, demonstrating in Jakarta last fall (1973) to protest the lavish life-style of the military elite and spreading joblessness, quoted from speeches Robert S. McNamara has been giving as president of the World Bank, not from Mao Tse-tung. It was safer to quote from Mr. McNamara, of course, but that was only part of the explanation.

AN INDONESIAN IN CALIFORNIA

Durojatun Jakit, a young economics teacher at the University of Indonesia whose lectures were said to have influenced the students, was asked about the origin of the doubts he had been expressing about the Suharto Government's development programs. Immediately he started talking about the Free Speech Movement, which was just getting started at the University of California at Berkeley when he arrived in 1964. Then he talked about seminars he took on development problems in Latin America that focused on the dominant role of foreign corporations and on mass unemployment and grotesque disparities of income.

When he finally came home in 1970, the young economist said, he had the feeling he was being followed by a ghost. "I saw a lot of the things we had been discussing in Berkeley–the extravagant consumption patterns, the unemployment getting worse," he explained. "There were more Mercedes-Benzes per capita in Jakarta than there had been in San Francisco. It seemed like a confirmation of all our theorizing."

There was also a new economic program that had been drawn up by an earlier generation of Indonesian graduate students, known as the Berkeley Mafia. Its main aim was to improve the climate for foreign investment.

Not at all radical by temperament, Mr. Durojatun started to express his doubts cautiously in lectures, and he soon had a large following. Later he found that the students had gone beyond him, that they were reading radical theorists who became fashionable after he left Berkeley and were saying that all foreign investment and aid should be stopped.

EVIDENCE OF DEMOCRACY

"I can't go that far," he said in December, but it didn't matter. In January (1974) there were student demonstrations at the time of a visit by Premier Kakuei Tanaka of Japan, and he was promptly clapped into jail. He has been there ever since.

The influence of the United States is not limited to abstractions. Americans traveling in Asia find that even the Vietnam issue tends to rank far behind television programs and fads in clothing on the list of things identified with their country. Sometimes it is even identified with democracy.

Kim Dae Jung, the South Korean opposition leader who was kidnapped in Japan last year by agents of President Park Chung Hee, was discussing the resignation of Spiro T. Agnew in the parlor of his home in Seoul, which was decorated with souvenir busts of Lincoln and John F. Kennedy and a certificate that named Mr. Kim an honorary citizen of Memphis.

"In Korea," he said, "Agnew would be regarded as an example of a clean official. To the Koreans it just shows that America is still the foremost democratic country in the world. Such things could never happen in other countries.

The observation led inevitably to the old question why the most democratic of nations habitually backed authoritarian regimes in other countries. In September, 1972, Mr. Kim said, when the United States refrained from any protest over the imposition of martial law in the Philippines, "I expected that this unfortunate thing would happen in my country too." President Park declared martial law the next month.

SELF-INTEREST AT THE CORE

Now in South Korea and the Philippines it is almost impossible for an American to have a conversation with opposition politicians without being told that the United States should intervene on behalf of democratic values. The standard American responses–that the United States has foresworn intervention under the Nixon doctrine or that authoritarian rulers are generally unimpressed by stern words from Washington–are normally dismissed as fancy rationalizations.

"You are already intervening here," said former Senator Jovite Salonga, an opponent of President Ferdinand E. Marcos in the Philippines. "You have your bases, you have your multinational corporations. If you're really against intervention, take out your multinational corporations and take out your bases."

Those Asian leaders who are most comfortable with the American presence take it for granted that the United States will act on a narrow calculation of self-interest.

The most consistent Asian advocate of the need to keep American power committed in the region has been Singapore's Prime Minister, Lee Kuan Yew, yet when he speaks of the way that power has been used, he speaks of American "ruthlessness."

Asked for examples in an interview, he was characteristically blunt. There was the Cambodia invasion in 1970, he said ("A whole nation of six million people put through the mincing machine"). And there was "the summary way the Japanese were cast aside" when the United States made its overtures to Peking.

"I'm not saying it's a personal ruthlessness," the Prime Minister added, "but there's a machine ruthlessness."

A CURTAILED PERSPECTIVE

Mr. Lee assumes that American economic interests will have to be served if American power is to be kept in Asia. . . .

American businessmen in the region usually say they hope to earn back their investment in five years. American official planning, which is still keyed to Indochina, seems to look no further ahead than two dry seasons there.

"What is the American picture of Southeast Asia at the end of the nineteen-seventies? How do they see it?" asked an adviser to the Malaysian Prime Minister, Abdul Razak, who has proposed that it be turned into a "zone of peace, freedom and neutrality" on the assumption that an American military pullout is both inevitable and desirable.

Official American comments on the proposal have been polite and noncommittal. By definition it would mean that the United States would have to withdraw from bases in Thailand and the Philippines.

Perhaps the greatest paradox of all can be found in the justification American officials commonly employ to explain why such a withdrawal is not a serious possibility. American forces were originally committed to the region to deter aggression by China; now it is said that China wants them to stay on to prevent a power vacuum that the Soviet Union might fill.

"I don't think any serious thinking has gone on in the State Department on these questions," the Malaysian official said resignedly. "I don't think the Americans have really thought through the question of what they will be leaving behind."

THE RELIGIONS

Only in Asia does the spiritual dimension embrace four historic, highly-developed and widely-followed religions–Hinduism, Islam, Buddhism, and Christianity–as well as animism and secular options.

This rich spiritual tradition contrasts with much of the rest of the world. Talk about religion in Europe and it involves Christianity and secular alternatives, including the quasi-religions of Marxism. African religions means Islam, Christianity or tribal rites. In Latin America the subject is Christianity and animism.

In this final section Alan Thomson looks at the various religious streams that enrich Southeast Asia. Each of them helps to define life for a significant number of Asians. Lee Soo Jin provides several "glimpses" of the church in all its diversity at work in Southeast Asia. And Feliciano Carino discusses the challenge to the image of the church in Southeast Asia; the challenge of the modern world and the continuing social and economic injustice so widely felt in highly populated Asia, is not simply to the church but to all the faiths that sustain Asians.

Finally a profile of the vital Christian community in Indonesia gives some idea of how a growing church participates in national development when it is a minority group.

THE RELIGIONS OF SOUTHEAST ASIA

Alan Thomson

The cluster of small nations called Southeast Asia has been the meeting place of the two great cultural streams of Asia, the Chinese and the Indian. India predominated, strongly influencing Burma, Thailand, Malaysia and Indonesia. China had a great impact upon Vietnam, and to a lesser extent on Laos and Cambodia. These external traditions are counterpointed by the indigenous Malay tradition dominating Indonesia, Malaysia, the Philippines and tiny Brunei (the aboriginal people of Taiwan are also Malay in origin).

The region has been the theater of operations of seven outside imperialisms within modern times; each has left a permanent imprint. Political pressures have also come from expansionist tendencies within the region itself. Moreover, each of the nations, organized more or less on ethnic lines, contains important minorities within its borders. Present boundaries remain fluid. Perhaps the one historical certainty for the region is continuing change.

Two great historical religions have dominated the region in modern times. Theravada Buddhism took root in Burma, Thailand, Cambodia and Laos. Islam predominated in Indonesia, Malaysia, Brunei and the southern Philippine island of Mindanao. (Only in Bali does Hinduism, practiced

---

Alan Thomson lived in Indonesia, Singapore and Hong Kong from 1961-1974. Born in China of missionary parents, he spent 1952-1955 in Iran serving under the United Presbyterian Church. After completing a B.D. and Th.D. at Union Theological Seminary, Alan and Jane Thomson went to Indonesia where Alan taught in theological seminaries in Java. In 1969 they moved to Singapore where he was director of the Foundation for Theological Education in Southeast Asia and taught at Trinity Theological Seminary. He has also worked for the Association of Theological Schools in Southeast Asia and taught at Yale Divinity School. His book *Worldwide* will be published in 1975.

widely before the advent of Islam, remain.) The ethnic Chinese–dominant in Singapore, strongly represented in Malaysia, with significant minorities in most of the nations of the region–brought with them traditional Chinese beliefs and practices in the form of a folk-religion.

At the base of these "high" religions as they are practiced in Southeast Asia, are two earlier religious tendencies, animism and mysticism. Animism is a religious answer to people's fear of the unknown and awe of the powers of nature. The animist deals with the unknown by placating or manipulating the spiritual forces controlling his nature (familiar to many in the spirit-worship of the early American Indians). Theologian Martin Buber has suggested that primitive animism is in a way more personalized than the higher religions, since it deals with nature in a personal way.

Mysticism is more humanistic in character, arising from people's sense of misery or alienation in existence. Mystics try to come to terms with themselves and their environment by an inner unity and integrity. Mysticism, including many animistic elements, seems to be the indigenous religious expression of Malay culture and continues to exert deep influence on the religious thought and practice of the Malay peoples.

The high religions on the whole have attempted to purge themselves of animism while being hospitable to mysticism. Although mysticism is the predominant strain in Hinduism and Buddhism, it is also found in Islam and Christianity. For the latter two religions the presence of mystical elements would seem to be self-contradictory. Mysticism seeks salvation within the depths of the self, whereas the revealed religions see salvation *of* the self as coming entirely from the outside. To put it another way, less sharply, mystics take the initiative in preparing themselves to ascend to God, whereas the revealed religions praise God for his gracious condescension to sinful humanity.

The one religious anomaly in Southeast Asia is the Philippines: three centuries of Spanish rule produced the only Christian nation in Asia. Thus, the Philippines is the one nation in Southeast Asia whose predominant religion is not East Asian in origin. In religion–and may other ways–Philippine life resembles that of Latin America more closely than of its Asian neighbors. Still, Filipinos are Malays; the underlying mysticism, as well as other Malay characteristics, remain visible. Five percent of the Philippine population is Muslim. And some animist groups exist in the highlands of central and northern Luzon island.

A number of minority religions are practiced in the region. These include the Hinduism of the Indonesian island of Bali, animistic beliefs and the curious indigenous sects of Cambodia and Vietnam which include Cao Dai, with a pantheon embracing Victor Hugo, Sun Yat-sen and Princess Margaret.

BUDDHISM IN SOUTHEAST ASIA

Buddhism reached Southeast Asia at an early date, beginning perhaps with the missionary activities of India's great King Ashoka. There are definite Buddhist remains from the eighth century. The Buddhism which came to Indonesia was later overlaid by the Hindu Shiva-worship and then by Islam. Buddhism became and remains the state religion of Thailand, and the predominant religion of the Indo-Chinese states (Vietnam, Laos and Cambodia) and of Burma. Burma claims to practice the purest form of Buddhism, and Rangoon was the site of the Sixth World Buddhist Congress, celebrating the 2500th birthday of Buddha in 1956. For the Congress a huge artificial cave was erected as the conference hall. The great Shwe-da-gon Pagoda in the center of Rangoon enshrines relics of the Buddha.

The Buddhism of Southeast Asia is Theravada, or southern Buddhism, and is closer to the teachings of the Buddha than is Mahayana, or northern, Buddhism, which reached China and Japan by way of Tibet. (Vietnam has both Theravada and Mahayana Buddhism.) In theory Theravada Buddhism is atheistic and nonspeculative. It is a method of attaining personal liberation in this world.

The essence of the world is suffering. Desire causes suffering. The way to escape suffering, obviously, is to have no desires, not to be attached to this world. The world is not a matter of interest in itself, but something to escape. So Buddhism does not study the world and has no cosmology or description of the world. When you are wounded by an arrow, you want to get the arrow out. You do not speculate on who shot you, or why.

The monk is the symbol of the Buddhist way of life. He has no property, no personal residence, no worldly pretensions and lives on charity. He eats what is given to him, and abstains from sexual intercourse. His time is taken up with study and meditation. He "goes through the world with lowered eyes," as Dr. Kosuke Koyama, a missionary from Japan closely studying Thai Buddhism, put it. Every Buddhist, perhaps as a young man,is expected to spend some time as a monk for spiritual training. A former premier of Burma, U Nu spent frequent periods of meditation in a monastery. The monk is a free person, exempt from taxes and military service. The new 1973 constitution of the Union of Burma denies monks the right to vote.

Buddhism has always been a very attractive religion, emphasizing modesty of thought, humility, gentleness, sympathy and charity toward the world. In its actual practice in Southeast Asia it is also intermingled with many animistic elements such as the veneration of Buddha's relics and the placation of spirits. It too is associated with ceremonies and celebrations, preBuddhist in origin.

Buddhism fears nothing from modern scientific thinking, since it has no cosmology of its own. It is in a sense a very "modern" religion, based upon a quite practical and undogmatic theory of self-integration and adjustment to the world. The problem comes precisely at the point of this adjustment. Buddhism arose as a method of coming to terms with a static and oppressive world, and static and oppressive were the appropriate labels for life in Southeast Asia up to the present. The present, however, poses a threat, since it is no longer static. Social and economic change present threats to Buddhist equanimity.

Dr. Koyama, in his book *Waterbuffalo Theology*, tells of traveling on a train with a monk who is leaving his monastery in order to open a bar in Bangkok. The American military presence in Thailand has changed things. The monk observed, "It is possible to make money now." The world of positive possibilities does raise problems for the Buddhist metaphysic.

ISLAM IN SOUTHEAST ASIA

Islam came to Southeast Asia not directly from the Middle East, but from Indian traders from Gujarat. Thus it came with a mystical element which proved very attractive to the local population. The evangelism of these lay-missionaries was highly successful. The first reports of the presence of Islam in Southeast Asia come from Marco Polo, who encountered it in North Sumatra at the end of the thirteenth century. It spread quickly as the competitor of the Christian imperialism of the Portuguese and Spanish and later of the Dutch. Islam was firmly established in the region by the end of the seventeenth century, and remains the predominant faith of the Malay peoples of Indonesia, Malaysia, Brunei and the Southern Philippines.

Southeast Asian Islam differs considerably from that of the Arab world since it came as the top layer to an already rich Hindu-Buddhist civilization. It was only in the nineteenth century that substantial numbers of pilgrims to Mecca brought back with them more orthodox forms of Islam, and also the modernist teachings of such thinkers as the Egyptian, Muhammad Abduh. It was thus the upper commercial classes who upheld the more rigid Koranic form of Islam.

The poor, who could not afford the pilgrimage, and the nobility, who had a vested interest in the status quo, remained loyal to the older, syncretized and mystical Islam. In Indonesia these opposed tendencies resulted in two groupings of Muslim political parties, a "conservative" and a "reformist" bloc. The conservatives were passive fellow-travelers of the Nationalist movement of President Sukarno after World War II, whereas the "reformists" supported the technocratic opposition, and their major party was outlawed. This schism within Islam has effectively prevented

Muslim domination of the government in Indonesia, in spite of a claim to a vast majority of the population.

The modifications which the indigenous mystical foundations brought to Islam in Southeast Asia were considerable. The figure who is traditionally considered to have converted Central Java, and hence Javanese culture to Islam, Sunan Kalijaga, is said to have done so after years of mystical meditation so profound that grass and bushes grew up around him without his noticing. Thus a Muslim was made without necessarily ever having heard of the Qur'an (Koran). Islam in Malaysia is identified with the Sultans, (rulers of states now within Malaysia), and so with a Hindu-mystical outlook on life realized also in the figure of President Sukarno. The ruler is the mystical center of reality in decreasing degrees. The function of the court is to stage the drama of inner harmony and the conquest of suffering.

As understood in its Arabic birthplace, Islam is severely monotheistic and not tied to the personality of its leaders. Islam praises the divinely revealed will of God as recorded in the Qur'an and submits to it. This submission is in terms of the clear-cut monotheistic creed: "There is no God but God and Muhammad is the Apostle of God." Animism has, however, reasserted itself even in Arabia in the exchange of Mecca for Jerusalem as the center of worship. There were no doubt commercial and perhaps tribal reasons for this. But the religious justification was the existence in Mecca of primeval sacred stones toward which worship was directed. Nevertheless, the sharp distinciton between nature and supernature is strongly felt in Arab Islam and generally denied in Southeast Asian Islam. The reality of a kind of Muslim unity is, however, an important political fact in the region. Indonesia is the largest Muslim nation in the world, and the former prime minister of Malaysia, Tengku Abdul Rahman, is the leading spirit and former Secretary General of the World Islamic Secretariat.

THE CHRISTIAN CHURCH IN SOUTHEAST ASIA

Christianity–primarily Roman Catholicism–is the religion of the overwhelming majority of Filipinos, and is also an important reality in Vietnam. Protestantism, to a lesser degree, is important in Indonesia, Burma and the Philippines.

The evangelization of the Philippines was the most impressive achievement of Hispanic Christianity and one of the greatest episodes in the history of Christian missions. The relatively greater success of Spanish missions in Philippines than in Latin America may be explained by the more compact land area, the absence of opposed high civilizations like those of the Aztecs and Incas, and perhaps especially the absence of gold or other portable valuables to distract the double-hearted conquistadores. The moral and social attitudes of the Spanish missionaries were on the whole quite commendable. (The one positive reference to religion in Gunnar Myrdal's extensive three-volume work on South Asia, *Asian Drama*, is to the educational work of Spanish missions in the Philippines.) The Spanish mission, however, was weakened by one fatal fault: a lack of respect for Filipinos as persons and a resultant deadly paternalism. The Spanish orders tended to keep the parishes in their own hands and to relegate Filipino clergy to the role of assistant pastors. No Filipino was consecrated bishop during the entire Spanish period. The first, the present primate, Cardinal Santos, was consecrated only in 1934.

The result was a church that did not take its role in the national life seriously. The Spanish friar, although admired for his many positive traits, became the symbol of imperialism, a chief object of nationalist resentment. One result of this unfortunate trait was a tendency toward schism in the American period. One scholar lists 350 distinct Christian bodies in the Philippines today, although more than 80 percent of the population is still Roman Catholic.

The most interesting of these schisms is the *Iglesia Filipina Independiente* (IFI), the Philippine Independent Church. The foundations for this church were laid during the Philippine revolt against Spain in 1896 and aborted by the American occupation in 1898. The chief of chaplains of the Philippine forces was pursuaded to secede from Rome after appeals for Filipino hierarchy were turned down. The IFI officially came into existence in 1902 with Gregorio Aglipay as Supreme Bishop. The church was highly nationalistic, and has been known to raise the Philippine flag at the time of the consecration of the host in the mass. At one time it also canonized the agnostic Filipino novelist and martyr, Jose Rizal. After some years of theological wandering, it associated itself with the Philippine Episcopal Church, which trains its clergy and helped to develop its liturgy, the Filipino Mass. Its claim to 1,500,000 members makes the IFI the largest non-Roman Catholic church in Southeast Asia.

The "main-line" Protestant churches in the Philippines consist of the six members of the National Council of Churches, the largest being the United Church of Christ in the Philippines with 350,000 members. These "conciliar" churches account for about 20 percent of Filipino Protestants, and have been active in ecumenical affairs. The huge majority of missionaries in the Philippines, however, come from noncooperating groups in America, including several varieties of conservative Baptist groups. Interestingly enough the Lutheran Church-Missouri Synod is a "conciliar" church in the Philippines, as it is in Hong Kong. None of the "noncooperating" churches is of substantial size with the exception of the Seventh Day Adventists, who are quite cooperative in the Philippines.

Statues of the Buddha, enclosed in each of the bell-shaped forms, top the magnificent ninth-century Borobudur ruins in central Java, Indonesia.

Some more extreme indigenous groups are of interest, including the ten Rizalist bodies who deify Jose Rizal as the God of the Malays. Particularly striking is the *Iglesia ni Cristo*, founded in 1914 by Feix Manalo, who is regarded as the Seventh Angel of Revelation 7:2. Manalo was strongly influenced by the Seventh Day Adventists, but found his own method of Biblical interpretation after a period of meditation in 1913. His church is a highly disciplined body which votes as a bloc and is much courted by politicians. The church buildings of the *Iglesia* are huge glistening white Disneylike structures which dominate their surroundings.

Christian missions, of course, are active throughout the region, but the church is only socially significant in South Vietnam, Indonesia and Burma.

About three million Vietnamese are Roman Catholic, belonging to a church that was built by the Paris Mission, a society of "secular" priests. Thus there is no parallel to the Spanish Friar image in Indo-China. French occupation was for only a century and training of indigenous clergy has been going on since the seventeenth century. The strongest Catholic areas were around Hanoi, but fear of persecution together with the perhaps politically inspired rumor that the Virgin Mary had left North Vietnam led to a mass exodus after 1954. The Catholic hierarchy generally supports the regime in South Vietnam, creating an unfortunate polarization with the Buddhists. The late President Ngo Diem Dinh was himself a devout Roman Catholic. Both Catholic and Protestant Churches, however, continue their work in the northern Democratic Republic of Vietnam, apparently without harrassment.

The Protestant churches of Indonesia, largely Continental-Reformed in mission background, are the oldest Protestant churches in Asia, and through mass movements in the last century now constitute perhaps 8 percent of the population. They are regional churches united in a powerful Indonesian Council of Churches which serves as their national voice. Indonesian Christians fully supported the independence movement, and have furnished important national leaders, including a vice-premier, a minister of social affairs, a minister of defense and two chiefs-of-staff. The smaller Catholic church has been active in much the same way. Both gained world attention by their considerable increases in membership since 1965 at the expense of the Muslim population.

A significant factor in Burmese life is the Burma Baptist Convention, which goes back to the missionary work of the American Baptist, Adoniram Judson, in 1813. Judson's Burmese Bible translation is still in use. This strong, self-confident, independent church is tribal in membership, strongly based with the two Karen tribes and other hill peoples. It has furnished significant ecumenical leadership, such as the scholar on Buddhism, Dr. Hla Bu, and the second general secretary of the East Asia Christian Conference, U Kyaw Than. The church is faced with an inherent problem due to its tribal character, especially since a number of the strongly Christian tribes are in revolt against the government. Wise national leadership by the Convention has maintained a cautious truce with the government, which is very sensitive both to separatism and foreign influence. Since May, 1966, only foreign diplomats were allowed to reside in the country, and since 1963, in practice, it has been impossible for Burmese to travel outside the country except on government business. The most universally respected Burmese leader, the late UN Secretary General, U Thant, himself chose to reside outside the country. Burma is the only country I know of where it is illegal to export the newspaper published by the Ministry of Information. The church has been well schooled in self-support and has grown since the beginning of its isolation. Burma also has a significant Roman Catholic church, staffed by Jesuits, Anglican and Methodist churches.

CHINESE FOLK-RELIGION

In Singapore, Taiwan and Hong Kong, and among the Chinese minorities throughout the region, the dominant religion is a curious blend of Confucian principles, Taoist rituals and Buddhist beliefs. Chinese traditional religion is strongly centered on the family, relatively unstructured and gives wide scope to private enterprise. Its most emotionally powerful elements are the Confucian family rites and the funeral ceremonies, but its most obvious manifestations are various forms of furtune telling and the search for good luck.

The Chinese adopt a curiously pragmatic attitude toward the latter activities, going from temple to temple and medium to fortuneteller seeking the one bringing the best results. Temples wax and wane in popularity. Various traps are devised to determine whether in fact the god or spirit is active in a certain place.

Clearly the element in this complex continuing to exert a strong hold on the community is the family unity of a mystical kind exhibited both in pre-Confucian ancestor rites, in Confucian principles of family conduct and in burial ceremonies. The family is seen as extending both backward and forward in time, and each individual is subordinated to the whole. To become, for instance, a Christian is to commit treason against the family system. The issue is not theological conviction, but social and personal solidarity.

CONCLUSION

Southeast Asia remains today a "very religious" region of the world, but a region in which this religiousness is threatened by economic and social change, by modern scientific thought and by political demands. Much of the religion in Asia has derived its power from its ability to aid people, to adjust and submit to stagnation, poverty and oppression. Originally Christian missions came with a liberating answer, but they came also with the assistance of the guns of imperialism and the other pursuasive techniques of world capitalism. Both are wholly negative factors in Southeast Asia today.

Southeast Asia is the meeting place, not only of colonialism and nationalism, but also of the high religions of the world. Real communication among these religions has come slowly, since evangelism thus far has been mainly among animistic tribespeople. But it is now beginning, and the fate of the Christian church, the Asian religions and religiousness itself is now in the balance.

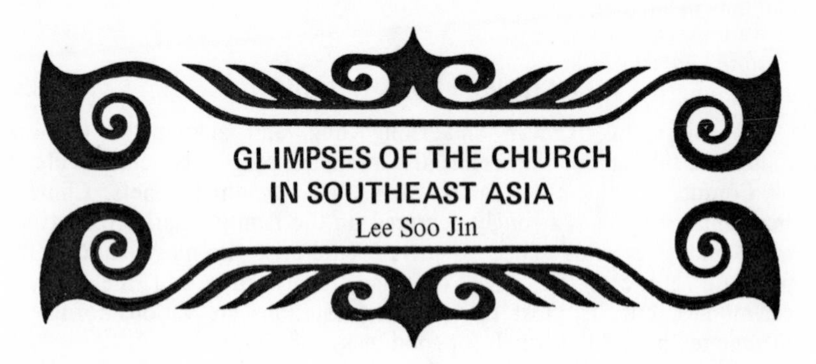

GLIMPSES OF THE CHURCH IN SOUTHEAST ASIA

Lee Soo Jin

"My father learned the lessons of life personally from his father, whereas I took them from books, magazines and television," said a leading Christian layperson in Hong Kong. "My wife, instead of listening to her mother about baby feeding, learned from Dr. Spock's bestseller. We are the first generation with this new source of knowledge–the mass media."

The reflections from Hong Kong are not uncommon to many Christians in Southeast Asia as they struggle with the meaning of the gospel amidst bombardment from the mass media, enticements of the advertisers and the sophisticated propaganda of various Southeast Asian governments.

What is the Christian response to the struggle for a meaningful democracy in Buddhist Thailand; to martial law in the Philippines; to the consumerism of Singapore and Hong Kong; to the continuing wars in Vietnam and Cambodia; to the sharp Christian/Muslim tensions in the Southern Philippines and to less direct but nevertheless continuing tensions in Indonesia and Malaysia; to the debate over self-development and the strong feelings for and against foreign investment; to a host of other secular trends and developments?

Anyone familiar with the Southeast Asian church knows that it has a variety of expressions and no single position would be possible on any of these questions. What is the church about which we are speaking? If we want an authentic understanding of what it means to be a Christian in Southeast Asia today, questions have to be raised. How free are Southeast Asians in the Christian community to decide for themselves their

---

Lee Soo Jin is communications secretary of the Christian Conference of Asia (CCA) and edits *CCA News* and *Asia Focus*. Mr. Lee joined the staff of the CCA in Bangkok in 1972. He is a graduate of the University of Singapore where he was active in the Student Christian Movement and national chairperson in 1971-72, while serving in the Singapore army.

priorities, their style of worship, their participation in the processes of national development inextricably linked as most of their churches and institutions are to the denominational and other vested interests of Western centers of Christendom in Geneva, London, Rome, New York? At home, how free are Christians from the ideological persuasions of all the "isms" so pervasive in Southeast Asia?

Whose views do we accept? The ecclesiastical leadership forced to try to maintain harmonious relationships with political authority, or the young seminarians increasingly pushing for a theological education that meets the human needs of their parishes? The congregational member who fulfills the weekly worship routine and perhaps tithes but who cannot relate to a Roman Catholic (if he or she is Protestant) or to a Protestant (if he or she is Catholic) in ecumenical worship? Or do we mean the Christian who prefers a more ecumenical fellowship with people of other denominations, not to mention dialogue with other faiths and ideologies?

As an Asian Christian, I have definite positions on many of the religious and economic and political issues being discussed in this book. But as an employee of the Christian Conference of Asia, the ecumenical organization representing some 35 million Christians in 16 Asian countries, I know firsthand of the myriad Christian expressions and differing responses to the Asian struggle. Nor is it easy to separate Southeast Asia's churches from the rest of Asia by any criteria.

Perhaps the words of Korean Christian Won Yong Kang catch best my fear of generalizing:

> In some countries, the situation may not call for exodus, but may be more like Babylonian captivity.. It may be either a priestly or a prophetic function through worship services, or it may take the form of underground witness. As long as we believe that the victorious history of Christ is ongoing in all the diverse situations in Asia today, we should formulate better partnership by understanding with good intention all the differing strategies, and with humility lend good advice and courage to one another.[26]

To be sure, such statements may remain the conviction of too few Asian Christians. But we can hope that the diversity of approaches in the Asian church may lead in fact to the changes that make for the new man in Christ.

What follows then are simply glimpses of various concerns in the Christian community in Southeast Asia. Each is taken from an existing document or newsletter. While the selection of these glimpses may reflect the prejudices of the selector, it is an attempt to show the diversity of interests within the Southeast Asian Christian fellowship.

PHILIPPINES

Muslim-Christian Reconciliation In The Philippines

What is the mission and role of the church in relation to the Muslims in the Philippines—the only country in Asia where the Christian faith is the religion of the majority? At a recent meeting of the Executive Committee of the National Council of Churches in the Philippines (NCCP), a Special Committee was created "in response to the need and the challenge facing the churches in the Philippines at this time."

The Muslim-Christian Reconciliation Study (MCRS) Special Committee has the mandate to implement "a comprehensive in-depth study concerning the mission and role of the Church in relation to the Muslims in the Philippines with special reference to the improvement of the social, cultural and religious conditions of the people of Mindanao." This would involve a review of the historical, social, political and religious causes and characteristics of the tensions and conflicts in Christian-Muslim relations over the years, and clarifying the part which the churches have played in bringing about the present conditions. It is also the Committee's task to "discover what the churches can do to remove prejudices between Christians and Muslims, and to foster better mutual understanding, respect and appreciation between the respective cultural and religious heritages of Christianity and Islam.[27]

Fr. de la Torre Heads Christian Liberation Group

In today's difficult period in the Philippines, explicitly Christian groups without doubt represent the greatest challenge to the powers assumed by President Marcos. One such group calls itself Christians for National Liberation. It is chaired by Fr. Edicio de la Torre, who says that the most authentic motivation for Christian involvement in the liberation struggle is the announcement of Christ in the Gospels: "The Kingdom of God is at hand, repent!"

"Shame prevents us," says Fr. de la Torre, "from immediately claiming a special place in the revolution, from immediately looking for leadership roles." He proposes that Christians see their role as "servants of the revolution." He amplifies:

> This is first of all a recognition of our inadequacy and our duty to learn not only from the masses but also from the Marxists. For our Christianity does not give us political and economic categories and other scientific tools to correctly analyse and solve the contradictions in our society. It is also the recognition that others have 'mastered' this task ahead of us and have the wisdom that only direct organized experience in the struggle can give. . . The Christian does not presume to have led or initiated the progress. He can only recognize, promote, criticize deviations. To be a servant of the revolution is to recognize the leadership of others in the revolutionary process without being servile (abdicating criticism) and

without being a servant of any ideology. The revolution is bigger and more creative than our inadequate attempts to completely categorise it. It is life. We Christians can hope that in serving this struggle, in risking the security of our present definitions, in the struggle for unity and in the unity through with 'strange man and strange tongues,' we will find meaning in the paradoxes of our faith.

> He who is willing to lose his life will find it.
> He who wishes to lead must serve.[28]

INDONESIA

Church Unity Consultation In Indonesia

A four-day Consultation on Unity and Witness was held at Sukabumi, Indonesia, from March 14-17, 1973. Sponsored by the Regional Council of Churches in West Java and the Council of Churches in Indonesia, the consultation was attended by twenty-five regional and national church leaders.

Dr. J. L Abineno, Chairman of the Council of Churches of Indonesia (DGI), commented that church unity in Indonesia has more or less been approached from an organizational point of view. . .the collection of church orders and liturgies from member churches for the purpose of comparison and adaptation. He suggested that the time has come to relate unity more closely to service and witness.

The Consultation sought to demonstrate that the challenge of unity exists in such common tasks as service, witness and Christian nurture. In addition, it sought to discover new expressions of unity, witness and fellowship–at the local, national and regional levels–and concluded by declaring that "the churches must have the courage to drop their own identity and accept and live in togetherness in a new identity in Christ."[29]

Development Strategy In Indonesia

What are some of the new dimensions for future cooperation in development programs between ecumenical agencies in Indonesia and outside Indonesia? A three day consultation sponsored by the Council of Churches in Indonesia wrestled with this and other questions relating to development in Indonesia at the Eastern Java city of Malang.

Dr. T. B. Simatupang, a chairman of the Council of Churches, suggested that education is needed in cases where pietism over-emphasizes personal conversion and fails to give adequate attention to human need, social justice and peace. "Rethinking is needed where churches see themselves only in ethnic denominational terms and not as part of the entire Christian community," he added. Cooperation with "other religious groups" is also of paramount importance.

"The church must learn from the poor, advocate social justice and help people find the freedom they seek without building new forms of dependence," said Mr. H. J. Pooroe, secretary of the Department of Service and Development in the DGI. "It must seek new ways of using its existing resources of people, experience, buildings, institutions and relationships in this ministry.[30]

WCC Assembly Bypasses Indonesia

The Fifth Assembly of the World Council of Churches (WCC), originally scheduled to meet in Jakarta, Indonesia, from July 23 to August 8, 1975, will now meet in Nairobi, Kenya, from November 23 to December 10, 1975.

Asian reactions to the shift of the Assembly venue have been mixed and varied. One of the first to appear in print was an editorial comment in *The Guardian*, an Indian weekly of public opinion, by Mr. T. K. Thomas, Literature Consultant of the CCA.

. . .Mr. Thomas observed that the "reservation of the Muslim majority in Indonesia (to the Jakarta Assembly) was deep and widespread and manifested itself in sad and tragic ways."

This "unpleasant episode" should first "administer a realistic warning to Christian triumphalism." Mr. Thomas was referring to wide publicity given in recent years to the large number of Christian conversions in Indonesia. "These achievements were held up to the world's admiration a little too prematurely and far too indiscreetly.". . .

The second issue arising from the Jakarta to Nairobi decision referred to the apparent communication gap between government and church leaders on the one hand and the Indonesian people on the other. "It looks as if both (government and church leaders) are out of touch with the fears and hopes of the people at large," he stated. Mr. Thomas went on to question the authenticity of the much publicized creative experiments in dialogue between Muslims and Christians.[31]

Indonesian Church Calls Korean Missionary

Korean pastor, the Rev. Youn Suck Kim, 35, has been invited to work as a missionary pastor at the Protestant church of Western Indonesia (GPIB). The letter of invitation said that the Rev. Youn and his family were invited on the basis of partnership as churches within the East Asia Christian Conference (EACC) to be a co-worker in the pastoral and missionary task of the Church in Indonesia.

The sending church is responsible for the travel cost from Korea and to the place of destination in Indonesia and monthly salary. The receiving church will be responsible for housing and program.[32]

First Indonesian Missionary To Holland

The Rev. Lutiko Handojo, 37, an Indonesian pastor, is going as a missionary to the Netherlands. A member of the Indonesian

Christian Church, he will work for several years in parishes of the Netherlands Reformed Church, beginning in April 1974.[33]

BURMA

Church Growth In Burma

"A total of 10,453 persons were baptized during 1973," reports the Rev. U Ba Hmyin, Outgoing General Secretary of the Burma Baptist Convention. "The Church in Burma may be isolated but not insulated–we are held together by a web of relationships made strong by love and kept strong by a tradition of one hundred and sixty years," he said.

U Ba Hmyin noted two trends developing within the Baptist Church in Burma, in his annual report for 1973. "The first is Indigenization or Contextualization. The judgements on matters of faith and morality in the days gone by and the creative innovations stalled by the leaders out of fear of syncretism will now suffer a bit. The indigenization or the attempt of the Christian faith to take root in Burma has to wrestle with the culture in which we were brought up, its values and concepts, symbolism and practice. The theologies of exclusion create barriers between the Christian faith and our cultures. Re-interpretation can create problems and also opportunities to enrich Christianity as we understand the situation more and more.

"Second is the emergence of deep emotional movements in some of our churches. The Byan-htan, or new-born movement, of the Chin Hills with its claim of special action of the Holy Spirit takes place at two levels, viz, the charismatic and the contemplative. Right now, the neo-pentecostalism movements stresses more on the Baptism of the Spirit, the speaking in tongues and prophecy.

"With the education of the Churches biblically and theologically the contemplative aspect will be an asset to the Churches. The church must meet the deeper needs of human spirit, in its teachings and rituals. As the church is by nature charismatic, the theological deficiencies and uncontrolled enthusiasm must be controlled and tamed within the fold."

The Burma Baptist Convention has 2,579 churches with approximately 277,000 members and 26 Bible Schools with a student enrolment of 879.[34]

THAILAND

Church Growth Conference In Thailand

Active Christians from all over Thailand gathered at Chiengmai's Prince Royal's College March 19-25, 1973, for a "Church Growth"

Conference, the second since the Church of Christ in Thailand (CCT) set its goal to double membership a little more than two years ago. Also participating were members of the Christian and Missionary Alliance, the Overseas Missionary Fellowship (OMF), the Pentecostals and the Southern Baptists which reflected signs of cooperation in areas of common concern.

The Conference reflected an increasing self-consciousness and a deep sense of mission among members of the Thai Church; well aware that they only number over 30,000 in the Protestant Church and some 150,000 in the Roman Catholic Church in a population of 39 million. More than 300 participants shared experiences of church growth programs in operation throughout the country and analyzed the common challenges encountered in the Thai socio-political and religious (majority Buddhist) context.

The Chiengmai meeting showed a flexibility to respond to the widely varying needs of Church workers from disparate backgrounds. The Churches in Thailand, both within the Church of Christ in Thailand and in other communions, have encountered different emphases on the role of Christian nurture as opposed to Christian conversion. In the view of one delegate, the Chiengmai Conference witnessed the common realization that the two concerns are part of the same cloth and not necessarily in opposition. "If we want to be a Church and not a sect," said one delegate, "we've got to learn to live with both functions."[35]

People's Organization In Thailand

During this century, the Bangkok (capital of Thailand) area has been experiencing constant urbanization. The adjustment of its citizens to urban life is an ongoing one but the possibility of accomplishing that transition is a real one, and it is here that the Voluntary Movement for People's Organization in Thailand (VOMPOT) is focussing its energies. Originally formed by a group of Catholics and Protestants, VOMPOT is a purely independent and voluntary organization committed to people often forgotten by governmental authorities in urban settings in Thailand.

During 1972, VOMPOT focussed on the Dindaeng slum in Metropolitan Bangkok, consisting of migrants from the provinces, evictees from other slums, and people with no regular income.

VOMPOT assists Dindaeng residents set up credit unions and cooperatives; it works with low-income families occupying quarters to which they have no legal claim.

The problems of these people are not simple; neither are the solutions. Who is responsible for the great number of slum dwellers? Who is responsible for helping them? If slum dwellers had the choice, would they continue to live in the slums? Are those of us who perform public services, such as tutoring children, distributing clothes, and providing electricity and better sewage for these people–are we really trying to eradicate some of these problems or

One of the creative forces in Southeast Asia today is the Christian Conference of Asia. Here the officers of the CCA assemble for a quadrennial assembly. They are, from left to right: Jurgette Malonzo, Philippines; Bishop John Victor Samuel, Pakistan; Henry F. J. Daniel, India; Won Yong Kang, Korea; Ronald O'Grady, New Zealand; General T. B. Simatupang; Bishop Yap Kim Hao, Malaysia; Francis Yip, Hong Kong; and Bishop Chiu Ban It, Singapore.

are we not? And are low cost housing projects really the best way to solve the problems?

The solution of a housing issue is finally only temporary. What really needs to happen is a change in the people themselves. They must have a new sense of purpose, a new sense of power. They must see that they have dignity, that if they confront the authorities on a question of justice, the authorities will have to listen to them.[36]

Asia Committee For People's Organizations (ACPO)

ACPO is a joint venture by Protestants and Roman Catholics in Asia, established in 1971, between the East Asia Christian Conference Urban Industrial Mission (EACC-UIM) and the Catholic Asia Committee for Community Organization. In February, 1973, the Office of Human Development (OHD) of the Federation of Asian Bishops Conferences (FABC) officially sanctioned Catholic involvement in the operation.

ACPO is the first, and so far the only, Asia-wide ecumenical action program. Its purpose is to assist in the formation of democratic people's organizations through which the poor have the ability to take part in the decision-making processes that affect their lives. Its rapid development since its founding reflects its response to three widespread demands of the times: international cooperation, ecumenical cooperation and the desire of poor people and poor nations to be free; or as the last Roman Synod on Justice stated, "to the arising of a new awareness in associations of men and among people themselves which shakes them out of any fatalistic resignation and which spurs them on to liberate themselves and to be responsible for their own destiny."[37]

LAOS

Peace Comes To Laos

On the eve of the Lao New Year, the leaders of the new Lao Government took their oath of allegiance to His Majesty, King Savang Vatthana, at the royal capital of Luang Prabang. This event heralded peace in Laos and it was welcomed by the Evangelical Church of Laos with great joy and happiness.

In a statement sent to churches around Asia, the Evangelical Church said: "We have all reasons to feel united with our fellow countrymen in welcoming the peace settlement as an end to the many war-inflicted sufferings of our people all over the country. Eighty of our congregations consist of refugees who were frequently forced to move in the events of war. Twenty of our churches were destroyed. We thank the Lord, who has given us peace and mercifully brought about an end of our long trials.

"We, the Laos Evangelical Church, hope with all our hearts that this peace will be a lasting one. We are a tiny church with forty ministers taking care of 17,000 members, but we are determined to actively take part in the new chapter of history of our people.[38]

SINGAPORE

Graduate School Of Theology Flourishes

The Southeast Asia Graduate School of Theology (SEAGST) has graduated six students since 1969 and enrolled some fifty-two students, forty-one of whom are currently working on their studies. They are doing this at a cost of less than US$1,000 for the two-year Master of Theology cource in contrast to US$5,700 for one student who studies in a seminary abroad.

Established in 1966, the consortium graduate school theological education is made possible because of the cooperation of accredited participating schools and the gift of time from faculty members. SEAGST is run on behalf of the Association of Theological Schools in South East Asia (ATSSEA).[39]

THEOLOGICAL EDUCATION IN SOUTHEAST ASIA

"We cannot and should not engage in theological reflection apart from the aspiration and frustration of the peoples living in Southeast Asia. Our people must occupy the primary place in our theological reflection," declared Dr. Kosuke Koyama at the Triennial Meeting of the Association of Theological Schools in Southeast Asia (ATSSEA) which met in Singapore, April 8-15, 1974.

"Most of our theological schools are too dependent on financial support from abroad," concluded his report. Since the majority of theological schools were founded by missionary professors, mission agencies responded to the needs of the schools. While this was a blessing, local Christian populations began to have the impression that theological schools can run without their help and support. Financial support is a strong symbolism of theological participation. Less local support means less local theological viability. This analysis must, however, be appreciated against the complicated historical, missiological, theological-educational, economic and personal backgrounds.[40]

ASIAN BAPTISTS

Conferring with the Rev. David Wond, Chairman of the proposed Baptist Fellowship of the Baptist World Alliance (BWA), U Kyaw Than, EACC General Secretary emphasized his own Burmese Baptist background and registered deep concern about the proliferation of 'confessional structures in Asia and around the world!'

Reiterating the views of the CCA that the churches in Asia could not afford, in terms of time, limited number of leaders, and resources, to cope with the pressing challenges that the churches must face in their struggle together in mission, U Kyaw Than advised that the Baptists in Asia be encouraged to struggle together in mission with Christians of other traditions. He spoke of the danger of each confessional body setting up conferences and parallel regional bodies dealing with similar issues and isolating their own members from others who confess the same Lord.[41]

THE ASIAN STRUGGLE

In the traditional period of the histories of our nations, the people were considered a passive tool to serve their masters; during the colonial period they were regarded as the object of economic exploitation; in the more recent period of independence and nation-building people have been treated as a blind force for economic growth. But today, having gone past a period of expectation and hope, conscious people are beginning to be awakened to the fact that passive expectation will not bring distributive justice and equal opportunity for all, but that the concerted effort of those who are oppressed and denied opportunity in bringing about constructive patterns of social change will be necessary if these dreams are to be realized.

There are, at the same time, congruent diversities of social and political realities in Asia which make a simple analysis impossible. But within this complexity we find several common social characteristics in Asia today.

1) The gap between the small minority of the rich and the large majority of the poor is widening.

2) International economic and technological expansion, which is in the interest of the minority ruling class, is accelerating the exploitation of the majority, often under the guise of contributing to nation-building and national development.

3) Increasingly in recent years, Asian countries are suppressing basic freedom of expression and people's participation in nation-building in the name of law and order, to maintain the status quo; it is increasingly difficult to distinguish between measures essential for the maintenance of law and order, and measures beyond, which suppress people's rights of self-expression.

The Christian Church in Asia, in the midst of these struggles, often finds itself too small and too weak, pitted against social issues that seem far too large for significant response. All too often churches are associated with the establishment rather than with the voiceless and the powerless, and are reluctant to lose themselves in the common struggle; and in their effort towards self-preservation they tend to forsake the masses in their need.[42]

THE MISSION OF THE CHURCH IN ASIA

What does it mean that the thrust of mission is now in Asian hands? What is our Asian understanding of mission? We find a variety of understandings each making significantly different emphases. Sometimes these arise out of traditions received, and sometimes they emerge out of the pressure of contemporary circumstances. Some emphasize mission as primarily preaching the Gospel for conversion and more dynamic church growth.

Some emphasize Christ's offer of the truly human, stressing repentance and the acceptance of the life style of Jesus over against the life styles one knows prior to the encounter with Him.

Some base their understanding of mission on the incarnation of Jesus, stressing Christian presence and identification with the needy. Through this witness the Holy Spirit may lead to faith in Jesus Christ.

Some, under the pressure of contemporary situations, understood in terms of oppression, say that the mission of the church is to identify with the poor and the oppressed (those who are at the mercy of others) and to create a community with the basic purpose of overcoming the powers which create the situation of poverty and oppression. They embrace the radical character of repentance, reject the inadequacy of the service approach, and express their faith primarily in political action.

All these groups draw heavily on the Biblical revelation for their faith and life style.

Mutuality In Mission

Since the mission in Asia is now in Asian hands, it is clear that the old missionary system must be changed to provide for greater mutuality in decision making, fellowship and sharing. Neither of the present methods most frequently used–namely block grants, or project method–achieve this mutuality of decision making. Moreover, as Asian churches themselves begin to send personnel and funds in mission, they are discovering that they may easily repeat the same mistakes of the West and re-duplicate the old missionary system. Many ignore the ecumenical channels, establish bilateral relationships, and set up paternalistic patterns. How can Asian churches relate to each other in more effective ways for mutual participation in decision making? However, due to the size and impact of resources this question is most critical between Asian churches and western mission agencies. As Asian churches, we face three knotty issues: First, how do we develop our own identity and a mutuality of relationships at the same time? Second, how do we develop self-reliance and inter-dependence together? The old patterns of relationships have proven difficult to break down. Finally, how do we achieve this true partnership? Some churches feel the only way is to establish a moratorium on missionaries and funds–especially from the West for a period of time. This is seen as a means to provide time to establish identity and self-reliance and to develop more adequate ways of expressing partnership.[43]

CHRISTIANITY AND DEVELOPMENT

Conscientization

Faced with the increasing injustice in spite of years of developmental effort in our countries, we realized that integral development of the human communities requires conscientization of the oppressed effecting the conversion of the oppressor. We felt that there is a gradual transformation taking place within Church organizations; every effort should therefore be made to hasten this process of conscientization from within, above all to institutionalize mechanisms of change. This transformation, though still restricted to a minority, has introduced a conflict situation within the Church. We felt that this conflict and the tension it generates is fruitful and limited objectives can be obtained provided this tension is accepted as part of the life of the Church and not neutralized.

This can only be achieved through a process of action and reflection and the organization of the oppressed directed towards surfacing latent conflict. Our role as 'Educators' in this process requires from us an identification with the oppressed. However our identification, unconscious though it is, is mostly with the oppressor as a result of our historical links with the colonial groups and the dominating social classes of today, our institutions which by and large tend to support and perpetuate elitist values, and our formation within institutions practicing an ideology of integration and compromise and built on a pyramidal model are obstacles to our identification with the oppressed.[44]

COOPERATION IN AWARENESS BUILDING

A small working group of representatives from the CCA, the Association of Christian Institutes for Social Concern (ACISCA), and the World Student Christian Federation Asia Office met in Singapore on October 11-12, 1974 to discuss areas of coordinated strategy and planning in the field of political awareness building and development education. Program units of the three have complementary plans of action and reflections within the Asian ecumenical scene and the need to pool their resources in a common strategy has long been recognized.[45]

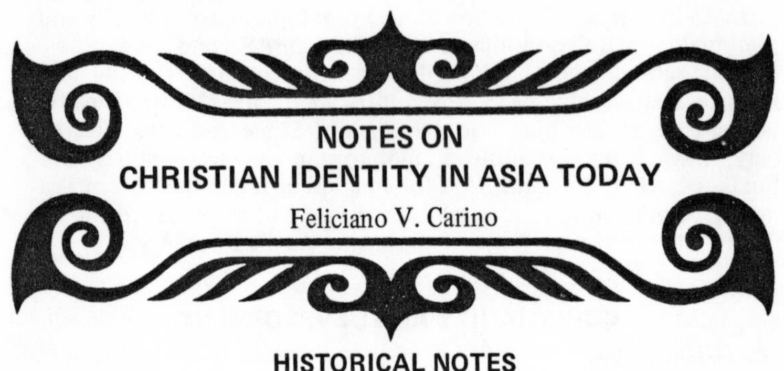

NOTES ON CHRISTIAN IDENTITY IN ASIA TODAY

Feliciano V. Carino

HISTORICAL NOTES

Christianity has had a checkered identity in the modern history of Asia. The Church must overcome a considerable negative heritage and

Feliciano V. Carino is the general secretary of the World Student Christian Federation (WSCF). During his student days in the Philippines, he served as study secretary and then chairperson of the Student Christian Movement. He holds a doctorate from Princeton Theological Seminary and this essay reflects his dissertation on the Asian church. Before moving to Geneva he was secretary for Student World Relations in the Commission on Ecumenical Mission and Relations of the United Presbyterian Church (USA). Teresa Carino, his wife, was general secretary of the Singapore SCM from 1970-1973.

come to grips with the social, political and economic struggles of today's Asia if it is to fulfill its promise.

Christianity did not come to Asia solely as a spiritual movement, as some assert, with only a religious message. On the contrary, its course of conduct from the time it arrived on Asian soil has left it with a dubious historical, political identity:

(1) Although constantly insisting on its autonomy and independence, it wedded itself to the dominating influence of the West, and permeated Asia under the protection of the economic, political and military power of the Western colonial forces. Christianity often provided a spiritual underpinning–a religious rationalization–for Western expansion into Asia. It has consequently been identified, therefore, as a foreign and colonial force:

(2) Pervaded by a naive pietism, it tended to reduce the historical oppression of Asian peoples into a religious problem. A vision of the "life-after" has often been offered as the ultimate resolution of the sufferings and agonies of the present. It has had little, therefore, with which to respond to the "materialism" of the nascent Asian revolt, and to grasp the religious dimensions of the explosive political, economic and social "materialism" in the aspirations of Asian societies;

(3) The dynamics of Asia's modern history–Asia's revolt against the West, for example–posed social and political problems. Prisoner of its own individualism, Christianity has been internalized, the individual isolated, and the relationship between God and the world reduced to a relationship between God and the soul;

(4) It has tended to consider the divisions between landlord and peasant, gentry and common masses, colonizer and colonized as secondary to the call for religious reconciliation. Divine grace is offered to all, as sinners. All are, therefore, reconciled to each other by the experience of a common religious predicament and the sharing of a common forgiveness. Thus, it has had little with which to respond, much less to give religious importance, to the dimensions of conflict present in current Asian politics;

(5) The aspirations of current Asian politics–indeed, of Asian politics since the turn of the century–pose a problem of overcoming the present, of creative tension towards the future. Too often Christianity has considered the historical projects of Asian political movements to be idolatrous, and the social and political aspirations of Asian peoples to be anti-religious, if not even demonic.

In the light of this history–many more points could be added to the list–a simple but harsh judgment must be made: Christianity has, at worst, played a reactionary, even colonizing, role; at best has provided an ideology of gradualism rather than of real innovation and social transformation. The result is clear. Although it has, at times, shown some utopian tendencies, and even flirted with revolutionary language and movement, and, in some instances, espoused some liberal causes and programs of social reform, Christianity at present has been deserted by the main currents of social and political change in Asia. A reconstruction of its historical identity, therefore, is necessary.

CHRISTIAN IDENTITY: THE HISTORICAL CONTEXT

Christian identity in Asia–as it is everywhere–has been and remains historical. Any consideration of a new Christian identity must be a qualified expression of a new and historical faith. This understanding requires a reversal of the usual way of interpreting Christianity: it is not possible, in this context, to start from "faith" and interpret things, or to start from "scripture" and apply it to facts, or to set the Church against the world. The process is reversed: "facts" illuminate faith, and explain and interpret the substance of history. What are some of the vital facts about Asia today that must illuminate the new Christian identity?

Rich vs. Poor

The first, and the primary one, must be: "why are there so many poor in Asia, and why in the midst of this mass of poverty are there a few very rich?" This is an obvious, yet often neglected, question.

As Asia's poor continue to be engulfed by misery, one point seems to be more and more clear; poverty is not just the first state on the way to becoming rich, but its opposite. The poor are not just poor, but they have been made poor, and are being kept poor. Poverty is the result of exploitation, of putting the poor in a perpetual state of dependence. The rich are not those who are at the end of a gradual process of development from the poor. The rich are against the poor.

Underdevelopment Or Dominance?

One cannot raise the question, moreover, about poverty *in* Asia without raising as well the question about the poverty *of* Asia as a whole.

Throughout the years of the "development decade," it has been asserted again and again that the poverty of nations is the result of the absence of certain "factors" which have been present in the rich nations. If only those "factors" are made available to the poor nations, they, too, will develop.

Despite all claims of development aid and technical assistance by the rich nations, several facts have become clear: (1) poverty has remained as the primary characteristic of Asia's social and economic life; (2) the economic and social inequality between and within nations has deepened; (3) the state of dependency and subordination of the poor countries to the rich has become greater; and (4) the autonomy and long-run capacity of the poor countries to grow have been reduced.

Underdevelopment as the condition of life of the poor countries of Asia is not just the take-off point towards development but has been the historical result of the development of the rich countries. Underdevelopment occurred in Asia as a result of colonization and exploitation; the development of the Western colonizers has created and continues to maintain the pauperization and state of domination of their former colonies. Development and underdevelopment are parts of the same historical process. To separate them is to deny the so-called underdeveloped countries their most recent history.

Freedom Or Security?

The emergence of militarism on the political horizon of Asia has multiple significance. Beyond the political machinations of military rule lie a number of presuppositions which constitute an increasingly attractive, but also often desperate, answer to the question of poverty and the development of nations:

(1) Development is basically an economic problem. To identify the resources and competences needed to develop require the skills of a competent and technologically skilled elite;

(2) In order to buy the time necessary to work out the complicated problems of development, stability and security become prime necessities;

(3) People are generally ignorant, their presence unnecessary and even disruptive;

(4) Within current Asian politics, only the military has the power and organization to insure both the stability and security necessary for the development process. Because, however, the military in the poor countries is not really strong enough, the assistance of the military in the rich countries is required;

(5) When development is achieved, the fruits of development will eventually, and in the end, trickle down to benefit all the people.

One can attack such presuppositions from many directions. For example, the stability and security so prized are also necessary to insure the continued dominance by the rich countries of the economic life of poor countries. In this light, the rise of militarism, and the support given to it by the rich countries, are the latest stage of the development of underdevelopment in Asia.

So in August 1974 Henry Kissinger, U.S. Secretary of State, defended continued American assistance to the repressive military regime of General Park Chung Hee in South Korea. Not surprisingly, he said that the requirements for security and stability in East Asia, especially for Japan and the U.S., superceded the requirements of human freedom and human rights for South Koreans.

Beyond the repression that accompanies it, the ultimate evil of militarism lies in its low regard for individuals. Human beings are primarily consumers and economic animals. Their victimization in the present is, in this scheme, not as important as the possibility they may have some new goods to consume in the future. This combination of military rule and technocratic development appears to buy the advice given by a Chinese sage to one of the ancient Chinese emperors: "If you want to keep the people peaceful, feed their stomachs, but keep their heads empty."

The rich, no doubt, presume that in the power which they hold, in their charity and benevolence, in the technologies they support and finance, in the political regimes they maintain, and in the investment of their wealth and ingenuity lie the sure pathway to the future.

The poor claim, on the other hand, that the future can be open to them only if some of these presumptions are challenged. The poor must be history's subjects, not its objects. In this struggle they must seek basically a more just and humane society, rather than simple prosperity. In the clash of these two views lies the future course of Asian history.

CHRISTIAN IDENTITY: THE PRESENT CHOICE

The new Christian identity in Asia will emerge not from any reworking of theology, nor renewal of faith and order, but from the choice made between associating with those who oppress or with those who seek to liberate and be liberated.

The luxury of neutrality is gone. It is not possible for God to be silent in this situation, and neither can the Christian. A call for a new form of Christian obedience must be taken seriously. It is the call to be clearly and unequivocally partisan with the poor, to be a Christian community in the midst of their struggle, ally to their cause and interpreter of their aspirations.

What this means in theory and practice will have to be explored with rigor and discipline. Certain lines of development, however, seem clear:

(1) Such a commitment to partisanship sharpens the Christian's understanding both of the conditions of oppression and of the possibilities of liberation. In the process, also, he gains a better knowledge of himself. The whole message of salvation takes shape in the search for those political conditions which bring and restore humanity to the oppressed. Salvation takes on a political dimension, and so does our neighbor. The neighbor is not just the poor ones; the neighbor also becomes the first and primary actor in the construction of a new man and a new society;

(2) For the Protestant Christian, in particular, this situation must push him to live out the prophetic character of the "Protestant Principle." Protestantism rose as an affirmation of the Lordship of God over the Church and society; its message posed the premises for their renewal (for the Church, certainly, a radical one). The fundamental attitude of the Protestant in history is not conservative but innovative, not repetitive, but creative. It is for this reason that the Protestant principle, rightly

understood, always stands as a guardian against accumulation of absolute power in history, and against claims for total allegiance and control;

(3) The Christian also must reassert more than ever before the character of the Christian faith as a religion of radical freedom. Christian faith is not to be described as a "religion of absolute dependence" in religious submissiveness (to use a term of the theologian Schliermacher), but as the "feeling of absolute freedom" in communion with the ever-active God, who will create out of the misery of his living creatures the Kingdom of his glory (a formulation of the theologian Moltmann). The Christian must affirm that, while man lives by bread, he does not live by bread alone. It is only through his free activity that he can really receive the fruit of the earth and find reconciliation with it. Those who offer man bread, but refuse him freedom, must face Christian anger;

(4) The reform of the Church can not be dissociated from the reform of society. There are people at the top of the Church hierarchy who would espouse revolutionary changes in the society as long as it does not touch the Church. But the reform of the Church can not be dodged in the name of revolution in society;

(5) Partisanship means action. Partisanship means that both its full meaning and its possibilities are explored in the act of participation in the struggles which the poor themselves organize rather than in the kind of thought and reflection away from action the Christian has become used to. Practice, not theory, is substance of this new form of Christian existence. To take this position seriously means that some very uncomfortable, controversial and disconcerting things must be said and done. Those taking this stance must have no illusions about the consequences.

THE CHURCH IN INDONESIA

Barbara Howell

Andreas Kebanga, stuffed into a crowded bus jouncing its way toward his home, talked with a bent and withered old woman sitting beside him.

This article appeared in the February, 1974 issue of *New World Outlook* and is here reprinted by permission.

He shared some bread with her; after she had broken off a piece, he paused to pray before eating his own chunk. The young Christian theology student explained his daily Christian witness: "I live with Muslims, talk with them, try to understand their lives. When they ask about the Gospel, I tell them."

Kebanga attends a theological school in Ujung Pandang, a southern city on Indonesia's orchid-shaped island of Sulawesi (Celebes). We were making the demanding 300-mile, 11-hour trip into the central hills of Sulawesi known as Toraja country. (An act of faith itself; on winding mountain roads the bus somehow survived the last two hours of night driving without headlights.)

The Toraja tribes possess a fascinating culture, manifest in boat-shaped houses beautifully carved with geometric symbols of an ancient religion, largely replaced now with Christianity, and a cult of the dead requiring bodies to be placed in limestone cliffs, watched over by wooden statues dressed in ordinary clothing.

Amidst the thousands of palm-leaf huts lining the road one had the word "Immanuel" woven in purple diagonally across its walls.

CHURCH GROWING RAPIDLY

Christians in the sprawling Indonesian archipelago always feel their minority position in the world's largest Islamic nation. Although only 8.5 percent of Indonesia's 130 million people are Christians, the church is growing rapidly, and its influence reaches most areas of Indonesian life.

Traditionally, converts to Christianity have come from animist backgrounds, but in recent years a steady flow of former Muslims has been baptized into its churches. This unique movement from Islam to Christianity is partly political, partly attributable to cultural peculiarities, and partly, according to many churchmen, explainable only as "the work of the Holy Spirit."

The unusually large movement of Indonesians into the Christian church in the mid-1960's continues at a slower but impressive rate in several regions, especially among the Javanese in East and Central Java, the Karo Bataks of North Sumatra and the Timorese on the island of Timor. Indonesia, an avowedly religious country, states a belief in one God as the first principle in the preamble to the Constitution. Religious freedom is guaranteed, though the community rarely tolerates unbelief.

ESCAPING COMMUNIST STIGMA

The mass movement into the church started with the tremendous political and social turmoil which occurred in 1965-66 with the abortive Communist coup attempt and the subsequent killing by the Indonesian people of hundreds of thousands (estimates are between 300,000 and 500,000) of suspected Communists and sympathizers. Many people probably rushed into the arms of the church to escape the Communist stigma. But perhaps more important, according to church leaders, after suffering those conflicts many felt an openness to a new orientation and a new commitment in their lives.

The Rev. Ardi Soejatno, moderator of the fast-growing East Java Christian Church, believes that most of the converts previously experienced some favorable contact with Christianity, perhaps relations with Christian teachers, nurses or doctors or with Christian neighbors. A former general secretary of the Indonesian Council of Churches, the Rev. Simon Marantika, tells of a man who gave as his reason for conversion, "I like these Christians because they are free, they enjoy life, though they live simply."

CONVERSION STORIES ABOUND

Stories abound of the "work of the Holy Spirit" in Indonesia, and Christians love to tell them. A group of students camping near the village of Madium, East Java, during a holiday period invited villagers to their services and became friendly with them. Later the village invited a nearby Christian congregation to instruct them in the Christian faith and most were baptized. In another instance a religious-mystic leader in Central Java suddenly announced that he and his 400 followers wanted to become Christians.

On a Sunday in June of 1966, 15 ministers baptized 2,000 new members into one church in Tigalings, North Sumatra. As recently as May, 1973, 500 adults received baptism at one time on Saleiar island south of Sulawesi. These and other instances of periodic spurts of conversions continue to be reported throughout Indonesia. The sometimes overwhelming numbers entering the church have caused problems for the congregations who already had too few ministers, but in most churches the need for additional leaders is met by a vigorous laity, by increased emphasis on theological education and by the expanding program of lay training centers.

ORIGINS OF CHRISTIANITY

Christianity came to Indonesia in the early 1500's with the Portuguese who established their Roman Catholic church while they exploited the treasured eastern spice islands. About a century later the Dutch replaced the Portuguese in the Moluccas and established the first Protestant church along with its colonial government. The oldest evangelical church in Asia now is in the Moluccas.

Christianity spread rapidly in the eastern islands where Islam had not been introduced, but Christian conversions were rarer in the pre-Dutch Islamic trading centers.

From about 1815 to the mid-twentieth century foreign missionary groups from Europe (mainly Holland, Germany and Switzerland) and the United States opened churches and nurtured the congregations. But with the internment of all foreigners, missionaries included, in the Japanese occupation during the Second World War and the subsequent struggle against the Dutch for independence, the Indonesian church was thrust upon its own resources.

After this dramatic break, the Indonesian Christians proved themselves completely competent to take up the work of the missionaries, and in the Indonesian Protestant church to this day missionaries fill only a few specialized posts. The Roman Catholic church has retained a Western-dominated clergy, though many of them have now become Indonesian citizens.

MISSIONARIES AND MONEY

The newer arrivals, mostly American fundamentalists and various sect groups like the Southern Baptists, who started their mission on Christmas day, 1951, depend much more on foreign missionaries and money from abroad in their Indonesian churches.

Although the Christian church began as an integral part of the colonial regime and was as foreign in its westernness as the colonial masters, Indonesian Christians were none the less Indonesian for their Christianity. In the first nationalistic moves in the early 1900's Christian youth groups identified themselves with this movement. Christian students were prominent leaders in the pressure for Indonesian independence as the Japanese occupation was ending. Christians like General T. B. Simatupang, who was Deputy Chief of Staff of the Armed Forces of the Republican army during the struggle, fought avidly for independence. PARKINDO, the Protestant Christian Party, was one of the first political parties formed in the new Republic.

A good relationship exists between the church and the Indonesian government. Christians' relatively strong leadership position in society gives them a definite stake in their country. President Suharto's Second Development Cabinet includes four Christians, as Ministers of Defense, Trade, Health, and Administrative Reform. Professional groups, business and the military have disproportionately large numbers of Christians, as do universities, almost a third of whose students are Christian. The two largest Indonesian newspapers are Christian-backed, one Protestant and one Catholic.

SUFFERING MINORITY STATUS

This does not mean the Indonesian Christians do not suffer from their minority status. They have always had to endure various forms of persecution in areas where a Muslim majority surrounds them. In the past Muslim hostility has taken the form of destruction of churches and Christians' property and a few killings.

Although this overt persecution has waned, minority Christian communites continue to feel anxiety, and Christian leaders encourage dialogue with Muslims in an attempt to ease tensions between the communities. In June the head of a delegation from the World Muslim League visiting Indonesia attested to their success by complimenting the country on its progress toward religious harmony.

Over five million Protestant Christians, the majority group, belong to the 42 member churches of the Indonesian Council of Churches (DGI). The basic goal of the Council, which was organized in May, 1950, to bring about the unity of the Indonesian Protestant churches, is far from fulfillment. The extreme cultural, ethnic and geographic diversity of the 13,000-island nation constitutes perhaps the main obstacle to unity. The Council urges cooperation in such common tasks as service and witness as a first step towards union. It also provides an opportunity for dialogue and co-ordination and carries out its own programs–from community organization, development and family planning projects to relationships with overseas Christians through the World Council of Churches and the Indonesia Committee boards in America and Europe.

MAINSTREAM IS CALVINISTIC

The basic theology of the Protestant mainstream is Calvinistic, with a pietistic leaning toward conservatism. Rather than denominational designations, most Indonesian churches identify themselves as either ethnic or regional. Exceptions are a small Methodist church and some Lutheran churches mainly in Sumatra. In some areas, especially north Sulawesi (where Minahassa is said to be 105 percent Christian), the Batak country of Sumatra, Timor, Flores, and Irian Java, the Christian church enfolds most of the population. The majority of Indonesian Protestants live in these areas. In regions such as Java the Christian community is a minority group gathered in congregations dotting the area among the Muslim majority.

Christian leaders are critical of the churches' tendency towards introversion, caring only for the interests of their own members. This stems from a traditional and still prevalent Indonesian tribal solidarity in which mutual responsibility extends only to the limits of the community.

Dr. J. L. Abineno, Chairman of the Indonesian Council of Churches, in his address to the Council Assembly in 1971 on the theme, "Sent into the World," described this tendency: "Many churches limit the world to the immediate world around them, the region where they live and have been rooted. People must leave the world (evil) to enter the church (good), and therefore they become closed and the church lives for itself."

CHRISTIAN STUDENT TRENDS

Christian university students, too, moved from intense political involvement in the 1950's and 1960's to a concentration on the spiritual life. Campus groups like Inter-Varsity Fellowship, Navigators and Campus Crusade attract many students today. The Student Christian Movement, which fostered most of the Christian leaders and was a political force, finds its influence waning in the face of a general student frustration over the government's refusal–until recently–to allow them a political role and the disturbing unemployment among university graduates.

Church leaders are working to shake Christians out of their insularity, to participate in a developing society. General Simatupang, a prominent Christian layman, told the Council Assembly, "Our participation in the process of development is very important so we can be in on the forming of a new society; so that the nature of development will be influenced by the church and an emphasis on social justice and the dignity and value of the human being will be given prominence."

Theological education in Indonesia, though strongly biblical, has been until recently unrelated to the problems of the local church and the world. A shift in emphasis has helped broaden the social awareness of theological students.

MATURE EXPRESSION OF FAITH

The Indonesian church, in spite of the overwhelming growth which strains its ability to instruct and provide pastoral and priestly support, in its totality constitutes a mature expression of Christian faith. One observer feels that the deep roots of the church in Indonesia's own complex culture marks it as a key to the future of Christianity in the whole region.

Before World War II, the famous Dutch churchman, Hendrik Kraemer, complained that "missions have continuously and with complete honesty proclaimed their own eventual superfluity, but in practice they have firmly imprinted on the minds of the people that they are indispensable. . . .Everywhere I found confirmation of the fact that Javanese Christians actually do not see the congregation with its interests, its needs and its growth as their own responsibility but as the responsibility of the missionary."

But when the war ended Dutch control of the nation and left the church isolated from outside contacts, the traditionally proud Indonesians proved to themselves that they could do the job. Indonesian churches are almost without exception self-supporting, and Indonesians occupy the pulpits of their churches.

Ecumenical activity and projects and programs outside the local churches must still find financing from abroad, however. One Indonesian church leader, when asked whether dependence on foreign funds for some projects would lessen local viability fumed, "Didn't the Dutch colonialists take our resources from us? What little money is trickling back is ours anyway!"

A VITALITY LACKING IN WEST

Now Indonesians view themselves somewhat like East African Christions; they have a vitality, a living dialogue between faith and life, which appears to have faltered in the churches of the West. Their relationships with churches around the world continue, but on a quite different basis. Clear Indonesian voices are heard and respected in ecumenical bodies around the world. Indonesian missionaries, like Dr. Harun who worked for Asian Christian Service in Laos for several years and then represented the Christian Conference of Asia (formerly EACC) in Bangladesh in the terrible days of 1971, themselves share in mission with other churches.

Indonesia's main Protestant bodies have a highly unusual relationship to foreign missionary influence. Dr. Alan Thomson, who taught in an Indonesian theological seminary for many years, wrote, "One is very struck in Indonesia by the lack of masses of missionaries." General Simatupang, commenting on the role missionaries now play in the Indonesian churches, said, "We invited the missionaries to return after the independence struggle, and they came into a situation which was very different than it was before. They had sense enough to understand this. We allot them a responsibility; they are not responsible for the church in Indonesia."

APPENDICES

Appendix A

Chungking
Ningching
Lhasa
Sadiya
Putao
Myitkyina
Mogaung
Shillong
Imphal
Bhamo
Mawlaik
Dacca
Comilla
Lashio
Mandalay
BURMA
Sittwe
Magwe
Prome
Rangoon
Bassein
Kyaiklat
C. NEGRAIS
G. of Martaban
Tavoy
Mergui
Tenasserim
MERGUI ARCH.
ISTHMUS OF KRA
Phuket
NORTH ANDAMAN
MIDDLE ANDAMAN
SOUTH ANDAMAN
Port Blair
LITTLE ANDAMAN
GREAT NICOBAR
Banda Atjeh
Sabang
SIMEULUE
NIAS
SUMATRA
Medan
BATU IS.
SIBERUT
MENTAWAI IS.
Padang
Telanaipura
MT. Kerintji 12,484 Ft.
Benkulen
Bintuhan
ENGGANO
Palembang
Telukbetung
Serang
Sunda Str.
INDIAN OCEAN
SUNDA ISLANDS
CHRISTMAS
COCOS IS. (KEELING)
JAVA
Jakarta
Jokjakarta
Surakarta
Banjuwangi
Denpasar
BALI
LOMBOK
SUMBAWA
Sumbawa-Besar
Waingapu
SUMBA
SAVU
ROTI
Kupang
OCUSSI (PORT. TIMOR)
FLORES
Ende
Dili
Flores Sea
Bonthain
Java Sea
BAWEAN
MADURA
KANGEAN IS.
Bangkalan
Singaradja
Ampenan
Bima
BANGKA
BELITUNG
Karimata Str.
Pontianak
Sukadana
Ketapang
Bandjermasin
LAUT
Kotabaroe
Samarinda
Balikpapan
KALIMANTAN
Makasser Strait
SULAWESI
Makasar
Kendari
BUTUNG
Donggala
Gorontalo
Menado
Celebes Sea
Tarakan
Tandjungselor
Bontang
Sarawak
Kuching
Lundu
Sibu
Bintulu
Miri
Seri Begawan
Bandar
BRUNEI
Sabah
Kota Kinabalu
Kudat
Sandakan
Tawau
SULU ARCH.
TALAUD IS.
INDONESIA
NATUNA IS.
ANAMBAS IS.
MALAYSIA
SINGAPORE
Singapore
Johore Bahru
Kuala Lumpur
Kelang
Ipoh
Kuala Lipis
MALAYA
Kota Bharu
Pinang (Georgetown)
Butterworth
Alor Setar
Pattani
MALAY PENINSULA
Songkhla (Singora)
Thakhoi
Kantang
Str. of Malacca
Gulf of Siam
CAMBODIA PT.
Chandaburi
Bangkok
Ayudha
Korat
THAILAND (SIAM)
Udon Thani
Nong Khai
Vientiane
Chiengmai
Moulmein
Pegu
CAMBODIA
Phnom Penh
Battambang
Siem Reap
Saigon
Phan Thiet
Phanrang
Nha Trang
Ban Me Thuot
Quinhon
Binhdinh
Quangngai
Hue
Quang Tri
Donghoi
Vinh
VIETNAM (N.&S.)
LAOS
Luangprabang
Hanoi
Haiphong
Ha Giang
G. of Tonkin
HAINAN
Kiungshan
Yulin
Kwangchow
Pakhoi
Nanning
Macao
HONG KONG
Victoria
Kowloon
Canton
Fatshan
Wuchow
Kunming (Yunnanfu)
Shunning
Tali
Likiang
BURMA ROAD
Kweiyang
Kweilin
Shenchow
Siangtan
Changsha
Kian
SOUTH CHINA MTS.
Shiuchow
Changchow
Chaochow
Amoy
Chüanchow
Foochow
Wenchow
Nanchang
Kiukiang
Ningpo
Linhai
Tung Ting Hu
Poyang Hu
Yangtze
East China Sea
Taipei
Chilung
Taichung
TAIWAN
Tainan
Kaohsiung
Formosa Str.
PESCADORES
Bashi Channel
BATAN IS.
BABUYAN IS.
C. ENGAÑO
Laoag
Vigan
Aparri
Tuguegarao
San Fernando
Baguio
Lingayen
LUZON
Manila
Quezon City
Cavite
Batangas
MINDORO
CALAMIAN GROUP
PALAWAN
Puerto Princesa
PANAY
Iloilo
NEGROS
Cebu
Sulu Sea
Zamboanga
Isabela
South China Sea
SPRATLY IS.
1479 Miles

This map of Southeast Asia has been sectioned off from the Rand McNally Imperial World on Mercator's Projection, copyright by Rand McNally and Company.

Appendix B

SOUTHEAST ASIA AT A GLANCE

COUNTRY	POPULATION 1975 Est. (millions)	LAND AREA (sq mi)	ANNUAL PER CAPITA INCOME	LIFE EXPECTANCY (years)	INFANT MORTALITY (per 1000 births)	ILLITERACY	MAJOR RELIGION	CHRISTIAN %
BURMA	30.2	261,790	$ 77.30	44	66	40%	Buddhism (85%)	4.2%
CAMBODIA	7.6	69,898	120.00	44	127	42%	Buddhism (90%)	1.4%
INDONESIA	132.0	575,896	96.90	44	125	40%	Islam (80%)	8.5%
LAOS	3.3	91,400	90.00	39	not avail.	75%	Buddhism (90%)	2%
MALAYSIA	12.4	128,430	422.00	56	29	35%	Islam (45%)	4.3%
PHILIPPINES	43.1	115,800	204.70	58	72	22.5%	Christianity	(80% Roman Catholic 10% Protestant)
SINGAPORE	2.3	224	1,216.20	62	21	30%	Chinese Folk (75%)	8%
THAILAND	40.5	198,500	202.30	56	26	30%	Buddhism (90%)	0.6%
VIETNAM (North)	24.9	61,294	90.00	not avail.	28	not avail.		2.6%
VIETNAM (South)	20.9	65,987.	175.00	35	37	35%	Chinese Folk	8.9%

Appendix C

Population and Per Capita Income in Southeast Asian Countries*

Data is for 1972 unless otherwise stated.

	POPULATION	PER CAPITA LEVEL (in US $)
INDONESIA	121.6 million	96.9
MALAYSIA	10.9 million	422.0
SINGAPORE	2.1 million	1216.2
PHILIPPINES	39.0 million	204.7
THAILAND	36.3 million	202.3
BURMA (1968)	26.4 million	77.3
VIETNAM (1971)	18.8 million	440.6

*Derived from *International Financial Statistics,* April, 1974, issue.

1. Peter Wiley, "Vietnam and the Pacific Rim Strategy," *Leviathan,* June, 1969. Reprinted by the American Friends Service Committee.
2. Dennis Bloodworth, *An Eye for the Dragon: Southeast Asia Observed 1954-1970* (New York: Farrar, Straus and Giroux, 1970), p. x.
3. D. G. E. Hall, *A History of South-East Asia* (New York: St. Martin's Press, 1968), p. 5.
4. Wilhelm G. Solheim II, "New Light on a Forgotten Past," *National Geographic,* March, 1971, p. 335.
5. *Ibid.,* p. 339.
6. Hall, *A History of South-East Asia,* p. 5.
7. Bloodworth, *An Eye for the Dragon,* p. 6.
8. Keith Buchanan, *The Southeast Asian World* (New York: Taplinger Publishing Co., 1967), p. 79.
9. Robert Shaplen, *Time Out of Hand: Revolution and Reaction in Southeast Asia* (New York: Harper & Row, 1969), p. 2.
10. *Christian Action in the Asian Struggle* (Singapore: Christian Conference of Asia, 1973), pp. 8-9.
11. "Philippines: Flourishing Economy," International Herald Tribune, September 6, 1973.
12. "Summary of National Survey of Major Religious Superiors," a twenty-two page mimeographed document.
13. *Christian Action in the Asian Struggle,* p. 13.
14. Charlotte Meacham, *Friends Journal,* July 1/15, 1974.
15. This issue of *National Geographic* contains superb photos not only of Pa-gan, but also the Shwe Dagon pagod in Rangoon (mentioned in the articles by Kyaw Than and Alan Thomson), the Cao Dai temple in Vietnam and Angkor Wat. The issue also produced a supplementary map with excellent material on the ethnic composition of mainland Southeast Asia.

NOTES

16. Translated quote from a Burmese publication entitled "Myanma Naingan-ye Khayee hnin Bogyokegyi Ne Win" (translated "Burma and General Ne Win") by Dr. Maung Maung.
17. Lucian W. Pye, *Politics, Personality and Nation Building: Burma's Search for Identity* (New Haven: Yale University Press, 1962).
18. *Constitution of the Union of Burma*, 1948, Article 21 (1 & 2).
19. *Constitution of the Union of Socialist Republic of Burma and Explanations*, 1973, translated from the Burmese Articles 21 (a7b), 22 and 147.
20. Pye, *Politics, Personality and Nation Building.*
21. Translated quote from the address of General Aung San, July 13, 1947, from the city hall balcony in Rangoon.
22. Reference: *The Specific Characteristics of the Burma Socialist Party Programme*, 1964.
23. E. L. Wheelwright, *Industrialization in Malyasia* (Melbourne, Australia: Melbourne University Press, 1963).
24. *International Financial Statistics*, April, 1974.
25. See *Second Malaysia Plan 1971-75* (Kuala Lumpur, Malaysia: Government Printers, 1971).
26. Won Yong Kang, "Asian Struggle for Justice, Liberation and Development," Christian Action in the Asian Struggle, (Singapore: Christian Conference of Asia, 1973), p. 29.
27. *EACC News*, November 15, 1973. (The *EACC News* was the regular newsletter of the East Asia Christian Conference, which became the Christian Conference of Asia in 1973. It has been replaced by the *CCA News*. Both are on file at the CCA central office at 480 Lorong 2, Toa Payoh, Singapore 12).
28. Jeffrey Abayasekera, "Theology in Action," available from Christian Conference of Asia.
29. *EACC News*, April 15, 1973.
30. *EACC News*, November 15, 1973.
31. *CCA News*, October 15, 1974.
32. *EACC News*, July 1, 1972.
33. *EACC News*, April 1, 1974.
34. *CCA News*, July 1, 1974.
35. *EACC News*, April 1, 1973.
36. *EACC-Urban Industrial Mission Project Reports 1972*, pp. 91-92.
37. *Ibid.*, p. 96.
38. *CCA News*, May 15, 1974.
39. *CCA News*, February 15, 1972.
40. *CCA News*, April 15, 1974.
41. *EACC News*, July 15, 1973.

42. *Christian Conference of Asia, Fifth Assembly Minutes* (Singapore: CCA, 1973) p. 51.
43. *Ibid.*, pp. 27-28.
44. "Statement of Asian Seminar on Religion and Development," *Impact*, November, 1973, pp. 371-372.
45. *CCA News*, October 15, 1974.